TO: My Spe

Mary D

The Politics of Tyranny:

U. S. Foreign Policy and Korea, 1958–1988

THE POLITICS OF TYRANNY

U.S. FOREIGN POLICY

AND

KOREA,

1958-1988

by
Dr. Woo Jung Ju

DORRANCE PUBLISHING CO., INC.
PITTSBURGH, PENNSYLVANIA 15222

ISBN # 0-8059-4817-1
Printed in the United States of America

First Printing

For information or to order additional books, please write:
Dorrance Publishing Co., Inc.
643 Smithfield Street
Pittsburgh, Pennsylvania 15222
U.S.A
1-800-788-7654

This book is dedicated to my wife Wook Ja Ju, and our daughter, Su Sie Ju, and to the memory of Dr. John M. Chang, Prime Minister of the Second Republic of Korea.

My education in the United States would have been impossible without the inspiration of the late Dr. John M. Chang, Prime Minister of the Second Republic of Korea

PREFACE

This book is a collection of my articles and letters to the editors of various newspapers over the last 20 years, together with statements by Senator Edward M. Kennedy on behalf of human rights and of democracy in Korea. My purpose is to clarify the dangers of the International Communist Movement and of proletarian, fascist, and military dictators. The strategy of U.S. anti-Communist foreign policy since 1945 has sown the seeds of serious advances of Communist expansion. The routs of political insecurity in the Third World are primarily social and political injustices under the iron hands of dictators, and the solutions lie in periodic free elections. It will take many years to change a situation whose roots go back decades. Meanwhile, the Soviet Union is constantly exploiting the unstable situations in the Third World by offering quick solutions to gain power over these oppressed peoples. It is as necessary to stop the Communist expansion as it is to bring about free direct elections. Then follow economic, social and political justices.

The way to stop the International Communist Movement is not to embrace fascist and military dictators; rather, the United States should promote the enhancement of human rights and democratic free elections as a fundamental foreign policy objective. Otherwise, she is likely to go down with the fascist and military dictators she is supporting.

Senator Edward M. Kennedy is the one person in the world concerned about the oppressed people of other countries, especially Korea. It is not interventionist to advocate human rights and free elections in another country. To promote human rights in foreign policy is more urgent than to maintain thousands of nuclear weapons.

Senator Kennedy took over as father-figure when his brothers, John F. Kennedy and Robert F. Kennedy, were shot down. Senator Kennedy has tried to spend as much time with his 29 nephews and nieces as he could. Senator Kennedy's children and those of his brothers are more important to him than politics. The Kennedy children admit that they owe a lot to their uncle. He is a good and solid family man.

Senator Kennedy is the heir to the New Frontier, and he will be the symbol of justice to labor, to minorities, to progressives, and to the feeble and elderly, the poor and the sick. Senator Kennedy owes nothing to any special interest groups; he is a free man. He would bring about economic independence, build a new patriotism, and solve the difficulties and problems of this land and in the world.

Contents

INTRODUCTION

The premises of U.S foreign policy have not changed since the Second World War, even though U.S. military and economic aid to the Fascist and military dictators have sown the seeds of serious advances by Communism since 1945.

Without re-examining the basic assumptions of United States foreign policy after the Second World War, every president has applied the anti-Communist Truman Doctrine, or doctrine of containment—in other words, of the Cold War—in all areas of the world, regardless of time and place and at great sacrifice of men and money.

The outbreak of the Korean War gave us impetus for the Truman Doctrine to spread in Asia. The Truman Administration acted immediately to aid the French regime in Indo-China, and dispatched the Seventh Fleet to the Taiwan Strait for the detachment of Taiwan from Communist China. The United States sped up the revitalization and rearmament of Japan and the conclusion of the Japanese Peace Treaty in September 1951. The United States' bold action in other parts of Southeast Asia included the signing of a U.S.-Philippine Mutual Defense Treaty and the Tripartite Security Treaty between the United States, Australia, and New Zealand in 1951. NATO became a full military instrument with West Germany and Turkey as full members. Following the Korean war, the United States had concluded four regional defense treaties, and maintained mutual defense treaties with forty nations besides. Nearly 500,000 U.S. soldiers had engaged in the Vietnam War, and there are still more than 200,000 soldiers in West Germany, 40,00 in South Korea, plus/U.S. military and economic aid to nearly 100 nations.

American support of dictatorships frequently works against U.S. interests: Batista, who, backed by the United States, paved the way for the triumph of the Castro revolution in Cuba; the corruption of the Chiang Kai-shek regime, also backed by the

United States, aided Mao's revolution in China; Diem and Thieu inspired the Vietcong in Viet Nam; the Shah of Iran led to the Ayatollah Khomeini's anti-American revolution in Iran; the Somoza dictatorship resulted in the anti-American Sandinista regime of Nicaragua; and El Salvadorans are rebelling against an absolutist government which the U.S. also supports. The United States never tried to understand the revolutionary changes in the Third World after the Second World War, and Communists are exploiting and gaining power over these unstable economic, social, and political conditions.

Since 1945, the Communists have never failed to take advantage of every crisis situation. Europeans leaders ignored Hitler until too late, and presently Western world leaders refused to believe that the Communists are really working hard to conquer the world. The world's Communist leaders have written hundreds of books and made millions of speeches intent upon destroying the free world completely. Lenin said, "We stand for permanent revolution" and "As long as capitalism exists, we cannot live in peace."

Nikita Krushchev once said, "I can prophesy that your grandchildren in America will live under Communism." Joseph Stalin said, "Can the capitalists be forced out and the roots of capitalism be annihilated without a bitter class struggle? No, it is impossible." Mao Tse-tung once said, "Every Communist grasps that political power grows out of the barrel of a gun... In fact, we can say that the whole world can be remolded only with a gun." In 1956, Khrushchev said in Moscow, "We will bury you," The Communist leaders have shown their true intentions to conquer the whole world.

The whole Communist movement has faced its own serious schism in the wake of its remarkable expansion since 1945. The Chinese and Albanian Communist leaders have become defiant and hostile toward the Soviet leadership of the Communist world.

The People's Daily, the Chinese Communist Party newspaper, on December 8, 1984 said: "It would be naive and stupid to cling slavishly to Marxist principles while seeking to modernize China, and if we continue to use certain Marxist principles, our historic development will surely be hampered." It added: "Marx died 101 years ago. There have been tremendous changes since his ideas were formed, so we can't use Marxist and Leninist works to solve our present-day problems." The Chinese Communist government openly rejected Marxism and Leninism, and certainly we know that Chinese Communist leaders never bow down to the Russians. The 1948 conflict between Stalin and Tito resulted in the expulsion of Yugoslavia from the Cominform. East Berlin in 1953, Poland and Hungary in 1956, Czechoslovakia in 1968, and Poland in 1980 and 1983 have rebelled against Soviet domination. The Vietnamese turned against the Chinese, a staunch ally and arms supplier during the Vietnamese war; and the question now is whether this will also lead to a war between Communist China and the Soviet Union.

Karl Marx failed to foresee the existence of nationalism in the Communist world, and misunderstood the whole of human nature. Under Communist rule, every aspect of one's personal existence was to be regulated by laws, children educated by government authorities, every form of luxury forbidden, and every form of individualism suppressed.

The whole aim of the Communist states is wrong since they seek not virtue, but only military expansion. The Communists are persecuting and exterminating all political opponents because they are always in fear of insurrection. The Communist system is not a good way to achieve real unity within a society. If property is held in common, no one will feel any proprietorship and thus no one will value or care for it. Human nature is not capable of feeling a deep interest in that which is only held in common. The destruction of the family system and of inheritance rights is impractical. Children will be recognized by their resemblance to their parents and children are heirs to their parents' property by nature. The idea of dialectic made Marxists or Communists look for a clash or struggle as the key to existing social institutions and the emergence of a classless society after the proletarian revolution. This is a whopping lie. The Communists are destroying the existing social system by revolution and developing and creating new social classes. Marxists or Communists are deluded that human and animal societies are no different.

Dissent, dissatisfaction, deviation, reform movements, and outright rebellion have come to the Eastern European Communist nations and to the Soviet Union. Intellectualism in Communist parties turned into a popular revolution against Communism and Soviet domination. The Communists claim that they represent the interests of the working class and enjoy the loyalty of the workers, but workers' protests against Communist rule have taken their most serious form and occurred most often in Poland and other Eastern European Communist nations. The working class in the Communist Eastern European nations has shown itself most resistant to Communist rule. Communist systems and the international Communist movement are in deep trouble, and contemporary Communism is very different from anything Engels, Marx, Lenin, Stalin, or Mao had in mind.

The government of Kim Il Sung's North Korea became more and more tyrannical in nature, and the people lived under a truly fascistic and militaristic communism. Every aspect of personal existence was regulated by law; individualism was suppressed; litigation was discouraged by a ban of written laws; children were educated by government; and the education was directed solely towards physical hardihood and military expertise. Kim Il Sung's authority rested upon mere force and suppression. Civil law rests merely on Kim Il Sung's authority, which establishes the standards of right and wrong within the government. The authority of Kim Il Sung always has the power of life and death over the people. Force and fear are the fundamental categories of Kim Il Sung's political philosophy. Therefore, the natural state of man is one of mutual fear. Kim Il Sung tried to unify the Korean peninsula with the methods and techniques of Mao Tse-Tung and Ho Chi Minh. Kim Il Sung's North Korean people are like the frogs inside the well.

Karl Marx had failed to pay adequate attention to the emergence of the institutions and practices of representative democracy. Marx never anticipated the resourcefulness and constitutional democracies. Marx knew 19th-century capitalism, but he knew nothing about the economic systems of the 20th century. Marxism was the old-fashioned, 19th-century, speculative, utopian philosophy of history, and has lost most of its appeals in the 20th century. Marxism may apply to animal society, but not human ones. All existing Communist nations are tyrannical or oligarchical in nature.

Proletarian, fascist, and military regimes exercise absolute power. The use of violence and police terror are institutionalized. Totalitarianism rejects economic and political competition and opposes the parliamentary system, popular democracy, and civil rights. It establishes one-party rule, develops a planned economy to replace the free market, stresses socialist and communitarian purposes instead of individualistic ones, and subordinates the individual to dictatorial authority. The government relies on single-party rule and depends on force to maintain power through police terror and repression. It subordinates all individual activities in the name of nationalism and subjects all groups, individuals, family life, the economy, school and social life to authoritarian control. The systems of Communism and totalitarianism and extension of their powers through the suppression of dissenters and the extermination of opponents.

Communist, fascist, and military dictators have not met, are not meeting, and will never meet their basic needs. Their governments are corrupt and corrupting and are attained and maintained through centralized power, absolute authority, bureaucracy, and terrorism. Totalitarian military elites have become a privileged and self-perpetuating caste. Milovan Djilas, one of the most influential leaders of the Yugoslav Communist government, argued that "the members of the Communist Party constitute a new political and social elite in communist societies, and this elite perpetuates the inequities of capitalist societies." The leaders of Communist nations have failed to create a classless society. It is a natural tendency of Communist totalitarian nations to produce neither social justice nor economic development, and none have met their proclaimed economic goals. Such dictators will never give up their powers, or even share them, without a fight. The Communist and totalitarian nations are twin evils, both dangerous and in danger.

Communist's nations continue to face grain shortages and declining industrial production due to their highly bureaucratic, centralized economic planning system. They discourage local initiative and disregard individual innovations. The standard of living in Soviet Union and other Communist nations remain far below that of free Western nations.

Despite the international Communist schism and fundamental economic problems, Communism are come to dominate more than 1.5 billion people in Europe, Asia, Africa, the Middle East, and Central and South America—more than a quarter of the earth's land surface and more than a third of the world population. Another 2 billion people are suffering at the hands of fascist and military dictatorships.

After the Second World War, the United States found itself in a remarkable position. It possessed more than half of the manufacturing capability of the free world and it had invested heavily in new plants. The United States controlled a near-monopoly in domestic and in many foreign markets. But the situation in the 1980s is quite different from that of 25 years ago. By late 1940s, the United States had half the GNP of the entire of the free world; but it had now fallen to 25%. U.S. economic growth has been slowing down while that of other countries has risen. Poor economic performance and the conclusion of the Vietnam war left the U.S. in its weakest position since First World War. Former Democratic Senator Mike Mansfield once said: "A new period is here, and we had better face up to it." Still, the United States with its enormous resources and productive power is regarded as the world leader and model of democratic government. I believe that strong leadership can restore the country's military might and global influence with strong economic foundations.

Senator Edward M. Kennedy, in an interview on Sunday, December 2, 1979, on San Francisco television, said he did not consider the deposed ruler to be a friend of the United States. I agreed with him completely. Since 1945, the U.S. has supported the most violent regimes in the history of mankind, and continues to embrace the deposed rulers. The United States has forgotten the price of liberty and freedom. U.S inability to come to terms with revolutionary changes against fascist and military dictators in the Third World has been a basic determinant of U.S. foreign policy since the end of the Second World War. This fundamental failure of U.S. foreign policy has created large-scale international disorders and domestic problems. For the last 40 years, the United States' support for fascist and military dictators has given the Soviets the advantage. It has put the Soviet Union on the winning side, while the United States backs rotten and corrupt regimes that end up losing. Each time a fascist or military government is overthrown, the United States fears the spread of Communism. This results in more militarism, more censorship, more deficits and more casualties.

The United States must use its power for righteous causes, but it must be careful to judge wisely. America is probably the first great power that could be called good. But goodness must not be equated with weakness and a refusal to take a position on right and wrong. The United States has lost much of the respect it once had. Even Britain and France criticized the U.S. over Grenada. American politicians, who have messed up foreign policy since the Second World War, are blinded to real dangers of the United States and to the world.

America should be governed by someone who understands power. Senator Edward M. Kennedy is almost a perfectly right on most matters of public policy and, as a politicians, is a cheerful, passionate and believing professional. Senator Kennedy is the heir to the New Frontier and the liberal tradition. Senator Kennedy believes that the basic test of government is how it treats the elderly, the sick without health insurance, and the poor without jobs. So he has always stood for job training, nutrition programs, medicare, medicaid and against big cuts in social spending.

Senator Kennedy has suffered enough from the Chappaquiddick event. Who do the press and reactionaries keep hounding him 20 years later after his infamous automobile accident? Nobody knows the nervous reaction a person experiences after such an accident, not even neurologists. People should study neurological research results before criticizing Senator Kennedy. Head injuries and shock cause victims to fall asleep, lose initiative, and fail to talk for a period after the accident. If a person doesn't like Senator Kennedy's progressivism, he should criticize his ideology. But please do not hound Kennedy for an unfortunate automobile accident over 20 years ago. Senator Kennedy works hard as one of the most distinguished members in the United States Senate, and evidently has the confidence to make the nation strong again. He has a convincing vision of the future and, once Senator Kennedy is President, everything will be all right. America will feel good again.

CRITICISM OF PROLETARIAN DICTATORSHIPS
AND THE WORLD COMMUNIST MOVEMENT

EDITORIAL PAGE

The Clarion-Ledger

R. M. HEDERMAN, JR., Publisher   **T. M. HEDERMAN, JR.** Editor
T. M. HEDERMAN Editor 1921-1948   **PURSER HEWITT** Executive-Editor

Page 10-A   JACKSON, MISSISSIPPI, THURSDAY, SEPT. 28, 1961

Dear Editor:

Having successfully applied pressure against the Soviet conspiracy in Berlin, this is no time to reverse ourselves and enter into a summit meeting at the United Nations or any o t h e r place. We have scored a knockdown. Now is the time to go all-out for the knockout. What some of the Free World's statesmen cannot understand are the reasons of the Soviet in seeking a summit meeting, preferably in Moscow. The Russian Communists need the conference desperately to recover lost international face, to regain prestige with their restive people, and to lure the West into a new period of coexistence and compromise.

The one significant fact involved in Soviet reaction to the American stand in Berlin was that the Russians did nothing. They blustered and ranted and raved. Troops paraded up and down the East Berlin's border with the West Berlin. But beyond t h i s propaganda outburst, there are nothing. To conclude that the Soviet restrained itself because of h u m a n itarian · considerations —because of not wanting to start even a limited war — is the height of the ridiculous. Communism cares nothing for the human element involved in war. Under the system of Red slavery, people are cattle, to be sacrificed whenever that benefits the system and its leaders.

Russia held back because it had to: because it dare not risk even a limited conflict involving its own people. Not even the brutal suppression of the Communists has been able to prevent the Russian people from learning who the real aggressors are who liquidated the Freedom Fighters

of Hungary and who is keeping those behind the Iron Curtain from attaining the individual freedom and the economic opportunity that they want. To a very large extent, the Free World has been frightened by a bogeyman, by the Soviet's calculated propaganda picture of hundreds of divisions, thousands of intercontinental missiles, and Sputniks whirling through space. Dangerous appeasements have been made in what Western statesmen term the interests of peace — wholly without realization that the Soviet cannot make war except as a choice of suicide.

What we need now is the return of Nikita Khrushchev's letters and statements — unopened. Let there be no summit, no negotiation, and just one communication, repeated over and over and backed up with the same kind of strength that has been shown in Lebanon and Jordan.

Once freedom has been restored to occupied lands and satellites — once the spirit of Hungary has triumphed — the Russians themselves will take care of their Communist masters. Discredited by its own members and already an economic, political, and psychological failure, Communism will collapse e v e n more quickly than it came into existence.

It is our firm conviction that in the long run Communism must disappear, even if we face it with weakness. Its own victims will destroy it, sooner or later, but the process may be extended and costly. The summit is designed to give the Soviet system longer and stronger life, to make more difficult the task of the Freedom Fighters. That is why we should summon the resolu-

tion to reject it, utterly and for all time, and then substitute an ultimatum of freedom and back it up with measures that will make its acceptance inevitable.

Woo Jung Ju
Graduate student from
Seoul Korea
Mississippi College
Box 781, Clinton, Miss.

The Clarion-Ledger

R. M. HEDERMAN, ˢR.,   **Publisher**   **T. M. HEDERMAN, JR.**   **Editor**
T. M. HEDERMAN   **Editor 1921-1948**   **PURSER HEWITT**   **Executive-Editor**

Page 8   JACKSON, MISSISSIPPI, WEDNESDAY, NOV. 8, 1961

Dear Editor:

In the Communist World, rugged, freedom fighters are engaged in a life-and-death struggle with the Communists. In the capitals of the West, statesmen are preparing to enter into foreign minister-level negotiations with Communism and perhaps even to go to another summit.

As with Hungary, Cuba. East Germany and Southeast Asia, those who are risking and giving their lives to battle Communism get nothing except a little moral encouragement. We wish them well or so we say, but for those who seek accommodation with Communism, we are quite ready to arrange meetings, to think of compromises, and perhaps even to enter into further appeasement.

This is precisely the reason why the Communists have been gaining and we have been losing. The United States and Great Britian supposedly believe the foreign ministers conference is a good idea because it has postponed showdown over Berlin. Yet we know of not one competent, informed, objective American or British observer who thinks that the Soviet Union will offer a Berlin solution that is acceptable to the Free World.

Delay might be wise policy if we were using the time to get ready for what the Communists have in store. But we are not. Time is on the side of the Communists. They are the ones who are getting ready; they are the ones who are becoming stronger and approaching the moment when they can risk all-out war. Negotiations with the Communists are futile and dangerous. Everyone with good sense admits it. But as in a Greek tragedy, we go on and on to a doom that we could avert but will not. We act as though the world were destined either to be plunged into another world war or to be surrendered to Communism without a fight.

American and British leaders say that they must talk to the Communists because their two peoples want peace. Of course they want peace. So do we; so do the peoples enslaved by the Communists. But the policies now being pursued are not leading to peace, unless it be that of the grave. Perhaps it is not true, but we think that some democratic leaders are misjudging the temper.

Development of the Berlin crisis found many Americans expecting a showdown and saying that it would be just as well to have it now. Nor can anyone who remembers the Battle of Britain claim that the people of the British Isles are lacking in courage and a willingness to oppose aggression.

There are many other indications that the people of the Free World do not want peace at any price. Probably their leaders do not either, but in continuing to talk with the Communists, they are running the risk of being trapped into another Munich. When a little is conceded to evil, it is too easy to give a little more, and so on, until evil triumphs.

The answer to the troubles of our time is still the same as it was when the Cuba, Southeast Asia and Hungarian people rose up against their slavemasters: to assist those who are fighting Communism, wherever they may be, and to have nothing to do with the aggressive system which is trying to suppress them.

The battle with Communism is being fought now; it is not an issue which can be put off to another hour or day. Let us stop the enemy first and then talk about terms. Otherwise we expose ourselves as hypocrites, and foolish ones at that, while inviting our own destruction.

     Woo Jung Ju
     Graduate Student
     from Korea
     Mississippi College
     Box 781, Clinton, Miss.

EDITORIAL PAGE

JACKSON DAILY NEWS

Mississippi's Greatest Newspaper

JAMES M. WARD, Editor   MISSISSIPPI PUBLISHERS CORP., Publishers

FREDERICK SULLENS, Editor, 1904-1957

PAGE 6   MONDAY, JAN. 8, 1962

Korean Speaks Out On United Nations

Editor, Daily News—One very important point is that the United Nations is not a world body in any realistic sense. Even worse is the fact that the United Nations can have no positive power because of the Soviet veto. That is bad enough.

Aside from debate, the passing of resolutions, and similar interesting but futile activities, what can the United Nations do? Resolutions did not save Hungary. Even now, denunciation of Soviet oppression of the Hungarian patriots continues to occupy the U. N. statement.

It is argued that this is praiseworthy in the sense that it constitutes anti-Communist propaganda. But if the people of the world have not yet awakened to what Communism is and what it does, can there be the slightest hope that another resolution is going to help?

We have said before and we say again, if the Soviet Union had not walked out of the Security Council just prior to the Communist invasion of Korea, there would have been no U. N. collective action to save this country. The Soviet would have vetoed it. Korea might still have been saved by Koreans and Americans—perhaps by a few other nations as well—but they would have been acting unilaterally and not as components of a world organization.

Of all the countries in the world, Korea has the least interest in undermining the prestige and the ideals of a unifying organization—one that has the power to keep the peace and provide absolute guarantees against aggression. But the U. N. is not doing this and cannot do it so long at the ultimate control—or negation—is in the hands of the Kremlin.

Our support and sympathy for U. N. objectives as they are expressed in the Charter cannot blind us to the fact that the organization has virtually b e e n destroyed as an instrument of a democratic, decent, and peaceful world. To pretend otherwise, and give U. N. allegiance blindly, is to evade the actions that must be taken to save the United Nations and mankind from complete Communist enslavement.

We are at a loss to understand the supine attitudes of Free World leaders. The Soviet veto has become so much a part of the U. N. machinery that it is accepted with scarcely a murmur, other than routine and almost polite dissent. Where have fled those great principles on which the United Nations was established? What meaning remains in the blazing, fearless words of the Charter?

Perhaps it is too late even now. Perhaps the United Nations is doomed to the fate of its predecessor, the League of Nations. Perhaps mankind must endure another bloodbath—horrible beyond belief in comparison with those of the past—before it learns that collective security is for all, and is not the exclusive possession of the aggressors, who protect their own and take from others.

Either the United Nations must be taken away from Communist dictation, must be set free to follow the oaths of liberty, or it is not worth defending and not worth keeping. Those who truly believe in freedom would do much better to leave it to its sudden or lingering death and join together with those of the world who will die before they accept the dictation of Communism. I believe in an organization of United Democratic Nations. It wants no part of a United Slave System.

Woo Jung Ju
Graduate Student from Korea
Mississippi College
Clinton, Miss.

EDITORIAL PAGE

The Clarion-Ledger

R. M. HEDERMAN, JR., Publisher   **T. M. HEDERMAN, Jr**   Editor
T. M. HEDERMAN   Editor 1921-1948   **PURSER HEWITT**   ecutive-Editor

PAGE 4   JACKSON, MISSISSIPPI, SATURDAY, MARCH 24, 1962

Dear Editor:

Biggest story in the Far East the world—is the smouldering belligerency of Communist China. It's a story bigger than Berlin, and bigger than any summit conference. Suddenly it is discovered that the nation with nearly 700 million population, which will have 15 million more people next year and 15 million more the year after that, and whose leader has boasted that China doesn't worry about atomic war because it could lose half its population and still have plenty left—suddenly, this nation throws overboard passivity in favor of the big stick.

What the U. S. Army was up against in Korea was the sudden change in the tactics of the Chinese Army. For years the Chinese Army had retreated when it rained, stopped for tea in the afternoon, never fought at night. But suddenly, under Communist indoctrination, they swamped American troops with wave after wave of screaming, howling sacrifice troops. Under those tactics, they had pushed American forces back from nea rthe Yalu River in one of the most shameful retreats in American history.

Whether the Soviet Union goes to the summit at somewhere, makes not the slightest difference. Danger resides not in the site, but in the fact of the summit itself. Khrushchev has agreed to attend for just one reason: to attempt to push the Free World over the brink. Knowing the record of the Communists in both negotiation and non-performance, how can we throw away our present position of strength and hand back the initiative that already has given the Soviet control of close to half of the World's territory and population? We cannot, and must not, if we are to survive in freedom.

If what is right must be cheapened or mitigated or set aside, then what good is right? When the aggressors and the oppressors refuse to stop using force to take what they want. Every time we yield a little, the Communists use that as a lever to demand and then to seize a little more. The end is obviously defeat for us and total triumph for Communism.

Woo Jung Ju
Graduate Student from
Korea
Box 781
Clinton, Miss.

The Daily Editorial Page

----------- Commentary -----------

Understanding Essential But Action Would Help

Understanding of Communism, including its intentions and its tactics, remains shockingly inadequate despite almost half a century of experience with its aggressive opportunism. This is demonstrated anew in the Berlin crisis for which dozens of tortured explanations have been offered. Some have said this is a showdown for possession of Berlin, others that it is designed to compel recognition of Communist East Germany, and still others that it is a feint to cover up preparations for an attack in the Far East.

The fault lies in the presumption that Communist moves are not part of a totality. Communism does not seek this or that; it is bent on gaining everything, or what can better be described as total power. When the communists attack here or there, it is always in furtherance of their world conspiracy in which the smashing of the United States would be the final step.

Attack Weakness

Communist's primary tactic always is to attack where there is maximum weakness. So it is that Berlin, which includes a free world enclave, has been a target before. So it was that Korea was invaded in 1950, and that the offshore islands of Nationalist China and India border remain under assault. In each case, the communists can be compelled to desist from aggression only if we reply with an e x e r c i s e of strength.

What will inevitably happen is the instigation of Communist pressure some place else, and subsequently-taking advantage of the concessions we have yielded in the place where tensions were supposedly relaxed. Berlin again proves that unless and until we make up our minds to fight communism with every weapon at our command, there is no hope of peace, and as year succeeds year, less and less chance of democratic survival. The old joke about those who lose all the battles and win the war is a fallacy; Those who lose all the battles do not win — they are defeated.

Reunification Sought

The way to end the series of Berlin crises is to take the necessary steps for the democratic reunification of Germany. The way to provide for Korean security is to unify this country, and the Formosa Straits conflict can never be resolved until mainland China is liberated and brought back to the free world.

Assumptions False

Protests that this would mean war are based on the false assumption that we are not already engaged in conflict. What, we wonder, are the shells blasting Quemoy supposed to be? Messengers of peace and goodwill perhaps? Similarly, the breaking of the Berlin agreements amounts to an act of war and should be answered in kind.

Once the fact that we are engaged in a war of survival is accepted, communism's piecemeal attrition will be immediately stopped and the objective of total power rendered unattainable. It is the only way. How many Koreas, Vietnams, Indias and Berlins will it take for us to learn this and thus prevent the nuclear holocaust that otherwise will be our lot?

Woo Jung Ju
Graduate Student in Government
From Korea

Readers Air Complaints:
Anti-Americanism Cited,

Dear Editor:

The United States is deeply concerned with the upsurge of anti-Americanism all around the world—and rightly so. Today the scene is the capital of Cuba; tomorrow it may be ten thousand miles away.

Because America is the Free World leader, this is not solely a problem for the people and Government of the United States. It is of deep concern to all of us who are dedicated to liberty and the defeat of Communism's drive to total power.

Behind all these outbursts is the devilish web that Communism is spinning in every country. Even Korea is not an exception. Here the massive infiltration of Communist agents seeks to discredit the United States as an aggressor and an occupier. Communism knows that if it can direct hatred against America, its own sins of commission and omission will be overlooked or ignored.

New solutions are called for, and it seems to us that they must be based upon p o l i c i e s of strength and firmness. America's prestige is vital to all of us; it cannot be expended lightly in the foolishness of appeasing those who have committed misdeeds and who deserve punishment.

The United States must use its power in righteous causes, of course, but it must be careful to judge wisely and in accord with the dictates of what will hurt Communism the most. America must realize that it is engaged in a fight to the finish, and that it must take off the kid gloves and strike back.

What we should have had was the wholehearted backing of the United States. It should, in fact, be a policy of the United States to require that any country receiving help outlaw the Communist Party, at least to the extent that America has done so. Otherwise, American assistance may actually be helping the Communists to achieve power. This is not a Sunday School picnic, but a war of survival.

America is probably the first Great Power that could be called "good." But goodness must not be equated with weakness and a refusal to take a position between right and wrong. If the meek had their way as things are now, the Communists would inherit the earth.

To counter anti-Americanism, The United States must have the respect of all nations and peoples, including the Communists, and it also must not be afraid to take positions that will be unpopular with the naive and the advocates of people at any price. This also implies the distinguishing of real friends from false.

—Woo Jung Ju
Graduate Student in Government
from Korea

The Daily Editorial Page
——— TUESDAY, MARCH 5, 1963 ———

Targeted by 'Bible-carrying activists'

Editor, Virginian-Pilot:

It is about time the American people woke up to what is really going on in Central America and other parts of the world. It is very dangerous that a majority of Congress and the media are so quick to oppose aid to the Nicaraguan rebels against the Sandinista government. This is another example of the Bible-carrying peace activists and Bible-carrying anti-American-activist tilt of the news media.

Anti-American activists criticize the government of the United States as hawkish and imperialist, but never criticize the governments of the Soviet Union, North Korea and Cuba. They say that the government of North Korea is legal, but the South Korean government is rotten, unstable and not legal.

They also criticize U.S. policy in Central America, but never criticize Russians and Cubans in Central America. They do not criticize the Russian invasion of Afghanistan nor the Vietnamese invasion of Cambodia.

They criticize U.S. human-rights policy, but never mention Russian human-rights violations. They never speak of the hundreds of hard-labor camps in the Soviet Union, North Korea and other communist nations.

They criticize U.S. nuclear weapons in South Korea and in Asia, but do not criticize Soviet nuclear weapons in Siberia that are targeting the entire Pacific Ocean.

Let's stop the activities of the Bible-carrying peace activists and Bible-carrying anti-American activists in the churches, campuses and public. They are more dangerous than the spies who are selling military secrets to the communist nations.

WOO JUNG JU.

Elizabeth City, N.C.

The writer is professor of history at Elizabeth City State University.

28

The Virginian-Pilot

ESTABLISHED 1865

RICHARD F. BARRY III, Publisher
CARL W. MANGUM, President
SANDRA M. ROWE, Executive Editor
JAMES C. RAPER, Managing Editor
WILLIAM H. WOOD, Editor

Published by
Landmark Communications, Inc.

FRANK BATTEN, Chairman
RICHARD F. BARRY III, President

Norfolk, Portsmouth, Virginia Beach, Chesapeake and Suffolk

SEPTEMBER 26, 1986

The dangerous drug war

To the Editor:

In search of commodities that the Chinese would buy, British traders finally discovered a very profitable product — opium. Opium, which was grown in India by the British East India Co. and brought to China in the 18th century, became an important item of trade in the 19th century.

Chinese administrators were troubled by the physical and mental weakening of the laborers, youths and military personnel used in the public works. These developments led the Chinese imperial government to prohibit opium imports. The immediate cause of the Opium War was the refusal of the British to cooperate with the Chinese government to suppress opium smuggling. The war lasted from 1839 to 1842.

The results of the war took away from the Chinese government its control over the Chinese economy, and the government was not able to prevent the forcing of Western goods on the Chinese people.

Communists are now conducting a drug war against the United States. It is the only way for them to destroy the United States, with its enormous resources, productivity and model democratic government. Communists are among those who are shipping thousands of tons of drugs to American people each year, harming secondary-school and college kids, government and industrial workers, and military personnel.

The United States must make an all-out effort to destroy the torrential supply of drugs and also wipe out the demand for dope. This drug war is more dangerous than nuclear war. If we can't stop the drug traffic, we will lose everything to the communists.

WOO JUNG JU
Virginia Beach

29

Contras need our support

Dear Editor:

It is indeed a sad thing on our times when all democratic party presidential candidates and the U.S. House of Representatives refused aid to Contras fighting for freedom in Central America. Without Contras, El Salvador came under the Communist hands, and Honduras, Guatemala, Costa Rica, Panama, and Mexico under the Communist subversive activities presently.

The U.S. House of Representatives rejected a request for $36 million in aid to the Contras fighting for freedom in Nicaragua, but the Soviet Union is continuing the flow of $300 million in economic aid and $500 million in military aid annually to the Nicaraguan Communist regime.

The Soviet Union gives 50 times more military assistance to Cuba and Nicaragua than the United States is giving to all of Latin America, because this Soviet aid through Cuba and Nicaragua to reach to entire Central and South American nations for the drug manufacturers against the United States and to the communist rebels to overthrow existing government.

The International Communists are now conducting a drug war against secondary-school and college kids, government and industrial workers, and military personnel in the United States.

If we can't stop the drug traffic from Central and South America, and Communist subversive activities in Central America, we will lose everything to the Communists without using a single nuclear weapon. If we do not wake up now, we will see the victory marches of Sandinistas and Castro forces in the city of Washington, D.C.

We must give up the wait-and-see policy and the policy of postponement of crises.

Woo Jung Ju, Ph.D.
Elizabeth City

30

The Virginian-Pilot

Serving southeastern Virginia and northeastern North Carolina.

WEDNESDAY ★
MARCH 30, 1988

Costly naivete about communism

To the Editor:

It is indeed a sad comment that all Democratic Party presidential candidates and the U.S. House of Representatives refused aid to the Contra guerrillas fighting for freedom in Central America. Without the Contras, El Salvador would come under communist control. Honduras, Guatemala, Costa Rica, Panama and Mexico are threatened now by communist subversive activities.

During World War II, President Franklin Roosevelt yielded all of Eastern Europe and the Balkans to the Soviet Union, but Prime Minister Winston Churchill saved Greece and Turkey, finally. If President Roosevelt had been aware of the nature of communism and Stalin, we would not have had the Cold War after World War II.

If President Truman had accepted the war strategy of General MacArthur, there would be a unified Korea and a mainland China controlled by the Nationalists. (In the 1950s, Communist Chinese forces had rifles but no tanks, no air force and no navy, and the Soviet Union had but one or two atomic bombs.)

If President John F. Kennedy had approved air support at the time of the Bay of Pigs invasion, there would be no Castro and there would have been no Cuban Missile Crisis in 1962, no communist regime in Nicaragua and no communist rebellion in El Salvador.

The Soviet Union has established military and political bases in Europe, Southeast Asia, Middle East, Africa and West Indies since the end of the Second World War, and now the seeds of international communism have been planted in our own back yard in the heart of Central America. It is simply unbelievable to me how naive some people are about the communist regime in Nicaragua.

WOO JUNG JU
Professor of History
Elizabeth City State University
Elizabeth, City, N.C.

31

"韓國에선民主主義가죽었다"

유엔本部앞서 一韓國靑年이示威

【유엔本部十九日発UPI=東洋】一韓國人은十九日「유엔」本部앞「유엔」廣場에서 李承晩大統領政府에 抗議하는 示威를하였다

賢憲民主主義의一員이라고 自稱하는「우정주」라는韓國人은「韓國에서는民主主義가죽었다」

라는「플라카드」를들고行進하였다 三年前에 서울에서왔다는 禹氏는 그는「유엔」代表에 南韓의選擧를 監視할「유엔」監視委員團을 派遣하도록 그들의關心을喚起시키려고 애쓰고있다고말하였다 그가 다니는「플라카드」는 李大統領이 武力이고든지 政治資金으로하고있으며 不正選擧를 實施한다고 非難하였다

MY BATTLE AGAINST THE TOTALITARIANISM OF SYNGMAN RHEE AND THE FASCIST MILITARY GOVERNMENT OF PARK CHUNG HEE IN SOUTH KOREA

KOREA

September, 1959

Dear Delegate:

Today, there is no democracy in Korea. The next presidential election is only eight months away. Syngman Rhee, now 85 years of age, is planning for a fourth term, despite his dwindling popularity. His hope for re-election is to expand his police power and dictatorship.

His record of coercion speaks for itself. In 1949 President Rhee imprisoned thirteen National Assemblymen. In 1952 he used the military to force through the legislature a constitutional amendment to insure his own succession that year. In 1954 he changed the Constitution, again illegally, in order that he might be elected president indefinitely. In 1956 he again succeeded himself for a third term.

Rhee has been cleared for the establishment of a one-party dictatorship in what is called the "Republic of Korea." His party leadership called 300 police to break the opposition Democratic party. After a 50-minute battle, the police succeeded in clearing the chamber of all Democratic assemblymen, and then locked them in adjoining rooms while his party passed the National Security Law without a dissenting vote on Christmas Eve in 1958, and passed a local autonomy law under which Rhee's government will appoint mayors and village officials instead of having them chosen by popular elections. Reason: Democrats had won control of every major city in Korea. It provided that local council elections will be held at the discretion of the president, which means there won't be any local elections unless his party is sure to win. It provided that the president will decide when upper house elections will be held. The Constitution calls for an upper house to the assembly, but there is none. Reason: Vice President John M. Chang, who would preside over the upper house, is a Democrat.

Evidently the people trust Dr. Chang and Dr. Chough Pyong Ok, (president of the Democratic party), and try to support them. Even under the police pressure the people have no fear of supporting Dr. Chang, and praise Dr. Chang's leadership for his becoming the next presidential candidate. My people immediately want to change the present government into another in order to obtain their security and justice. They can accomplish this only by being guaranteed free and honest elections.

My people believe that only the United Nations can redress their grievances. My people ask that the United States government and the United Nations watch the ballot box in Korea closely. My people earnestly hope that the United Nations will understand this fact, that the United Nations can break the dictatorship of Rhee's administration and give the people of Korea the democratic government that they so earnestly desire.

In order to guarantee to the people of Korea a truly democratic election, the UNITED NATIONS MUST SEND A UNITED NATIONS SURVEILLANCE COMMITTEE to observe the elections. This will be necessary to insure that the elections are carried out in a manner befitting a free people.

I call upon you in the name of freedom to help my people again in their fight for freedom. The United Nations saved Korea from a totalitarianism imposed from without her country. I beg you to save her from this totalitarianism being imposed from within.

Woo Jung Ju
Delegate of the Petitioners
The Republic of Korea

34

Sam Rayburn, Speaker of the U.S. House of Representatives, his home, Bonham, Texas 1960

LYNDON B. JOHNSON
TEXAS

United States Senate
Office of the Democratic Leader
Washington, D. C.

September 2, 1959

My dear Friend:

I appreciate your thoughtfulness in for-
warding to me your petition addressed
to the United Nations and asking creation
of a U. N. Surveillance Committee to
observe elections in Korea. I'm glad
to have the benefit of your thinking.

Sincerely,

Lyndon B. Johnson

Mr. Woo Jung Ju
Box 3002 E. T. Station
Commerce, Texas

UNITED STATES DEPARTMENT OF JUSTICE
IMMIGRATION AND NATURALIZATION SERVICE
WASHINGTON 25, D. C.

PLEASE ADDRESS REPLY TO

OFFICE OF THE COMMISSIONER

MAR 3 1 1960

AND REFER TO THIS FILE NO:
CO 703.164

Dear Mr. Rayburn:

Further reference is made to your letter of March 11, 1960, with which you enclosed a communication from Mr. Woo Jung Ju concerning his desire to remain in the United States.

Mr. Ju was admitted to the United States as a student on February 10, 1957, and his stay was last extended to April 11, 1960.

Mr. Ju enrolled in Oregon State College in 1957 and during January 1959 terminated his attendance there and, without the permission of this Service, went to Commerce, Texas and enrolled in East Texas State College. His case was carefully considered by the Service at that time and he was granted an extension of stay to April 11, 1960. During the summer of 1959 he withdrew from East Texas State College and efforts to locate him in New York and Washington, D. C. were unsuccessful.

Mr. Ju was located at East Texas State College on March 5, 1960. Although he is auditing some classes he is not enrolled in the college and is financially unable to do so. He claims he will borrow the necessary funds to enroll in school. His passport was cancelled by the Korean Consul General in San Francisco on September 30, 1959.

The District Director of this Service at Dallas, Texas has informed Mr. Ju that if he can secure an extension of his passport and enroll in an approved school further consideration will be given to permitting him to resume the status of a student.

When further action is taken in this case you will be advised.

Sincerely,

Commissioner

Enclosure

Honorable Sam Rayburn
House of Representatives
Washington, D. C.

37

Dr. Syngman Rhee Loses, His Popularity

To the Editor:

It is quite an obvious fact today that the Korean people are gradually appreciating Dr. John M. Chang's leadership (the vice president of the Republic of Korea) as well as his personality, which is measured better than Dr. Syngman Rhee's leadership. For over the majority of the Korean people do so. Today the Korean people focus their attention to this new phase of change.

The Korean people regard Dr. Syngman Rhee as a disguised dictatorial politician who is struggling for power. Dr. Rhee is a well known politician, who often abuses the Constitution of the Republic of Korea, the "Law of the Land." Many Korean people frequently say that the power of Dr. Rhee is above the Constitution. That is to say, Dr. Rhee's politics is primarily based upon force (police and military) rather than public opinion. His leadership puts force ahead and the public opinion secondary. Moreover, the continuously increasing economic unrest causes the people to look upon the government as a reluctant stool. Furthermore, the present government lost its faith on the issue of the unification; the people hesitate to believe even the new issues.

Dr. Chang, on the other hand, who is one of the top political machine of the Democratic party, is getting the popularity. For the people realize his pious and capable personality as well as his leadership. Evidently the people trust Dr. Chang and try to support him. Even under the police pressure the people have less fear supporting Dr. Chang.

The majority of the college students and the minor parties together praise Dr. Chang's leadership for this coming next presidential candidate. In the last election, May 5, 1956, for the vice presidential campaign, Dr. Chang beat Mr. Lee Ki Bong, who was nominated by Dr. Rhee as the vice presidential candidate. This favor in popularity of Dr. Chang is increasing day by day.

The Korean people recognize that the present government ignores the police interference with the private activities and their terror activities, which directly prohibit the freedom of speech, the freedom of assembly, and even, to some extent, the freedom of the press. As a practical example, while I was serving as a chief campaign manager for Dr. Chang, who was vice presidential candidate in the Seoul district, in May of 1956, my office was covered by gas and burned up by about 13 members of the terror group in the middle of the day in Seoul. It was just five days before the election day. After that there was no special city or government arrangement for my office at all. Moreover, Dr. Chang, was shot in his right hand by a terrorist at the Democratic general convention in Seoul.

Under these circumstances, the Korean people are well aware of what they are supposed to do. They immediately want to change the present government into another in order to obtain their security and justice. Indeed this is the real Korean public opinion of today.

It should be a regrettable fact that Dr. Rhee once mentioned to a reporter of the Agency France Press on July 18, 1957, that Chang's party, the Democratic party, is just like a Communistic party. The Korean people, especially intellectual groups, see this fact that Dr. Rhee always attacks this way if anyone of the party or any group as well as an individual opposes his leadership. The majority of the people do hope for a somewhat new and changeable government so that they are able to get their security as well as enjoyment.

> Woo Jung Ju,
> Oregon State college
> student of Seoul, Korea

THE DAILY BAROMETER

Oregon State University, Corvallis, Oregon

January 1958

By WOO JUNG JU

If the congressional election of May, 1958, is held in a free environment, the Democratic party in Korea will win 200 of 233 fixed seats in the Korean national assembly.

The following factors assure the victory of the Democratic party in coming election. On May 5, 1956, Ik Hee Shin (a witty speaker in the Korean house of representatives since the beginning of that constitutional assembly) had an overwhelming popularity among the people when he ran for the presidency of the Republic of Korea. Had he not died 10 days before the election, he would have been elected.

In spite of the police terror of Liberal party (President Synghman Rhee's party) administration in that election, the Korean people, who hated the long period of dictatorial and bureaucratic administration of the Liberal party, elected the Democratic party vice-presidential candidate, Dr. John M. Chang.

Moreover, in the election of Seoul city assembly in August, 1956, the Democratic party won 40 of the 47 seats by an overwhelming majority. Only two seats were given to the governmental party candidates.

When we examine the speech campaign item in the election law, which has recently passed the national assembly, the coming May election will be even more interfered with and suppressed by the present administration. Then, what is the significance of May election? It does not mean the instant substitution of the present administration.

Under the British model constitution, the parliamentary elections determine the administration as well as the legislature. But under the U.S. modeled Korean constitution, the change of the administration is largely determined by the four-year period of the presidential office term. The present Korean presidential term of office will end in August 1960. Accordingly practical power of present Korean administration will continue regardless of a victory of an opposition party.

But if the Democratic party wins a majority of more than two third of the seats in the assembly the situation will change a little. The Democratic party will try to substitute the presidential system of government with a cabinet system of government through a constitutional amendment. This is one of the possible ways of changing the present administration. But the present suppression system will prevent a victory for the Democratic party in this coming election.

On the contrary, if the Liberal party, which is the governmental party, wins in May election, they will also try to amend the present constitution, but in a different way. The Liberal party members have been attempting to cut off, the succession right of the vice-president, in case of the absence of the president.

This attempt was not successful in the present assembly, but if the Liberal party wins a two-thirds majority in the May election, they will amend the constitution for the purpose of curbing the vice-presidential rights. Moreover, they will try to amend the presidential election law from direct popular elections into indirect congressional election. Thus, the Liberal party will put forth a supreme effort to maintain their power permanently.

Accordingly, the future Korean political situation will be largely determined by the May election. The fixed number of seats in the house of representatives is 233 (an exact majority of 233 is 155½. Thus, according to which rule is applied, either 155 or 156 will constitute a majority.) Consequently, 78 (79) is the minimum number which the opposition party needs to prevent the passing of a constitutional amendment.

In view of this, the significance of May election lies not in the victory of the opposition party, but on the power of the Liberal party to prevent the passing of an amendment to the constitution. By and large, Korean people are well aware of this situation and will stop this attempt of the government party by exercising their voting power.

THE DAILY BAROMETER

Oregon State University, Corvallis, Oregon

39

The Daily Editorial Page

On Korea,

Dear Editor.

Freedom is gone in the Republic of Korea. A handful of generals with a monopoly of force — supported by the many who believe that Korea is unsuited or unprepared for democracy, tolerated by an apathetic or intimidated majority, and opposed by virtually no one — has established a military dictatorship.

The late free Korea was an obviously sick but perceptibly improving society. Its main diseases — corruption, factionalism, irresponsibility and poverty — were diagnosed and lamented by a free political forum, a free press, a free academic community and a free citizenry, all suffering from the same ills.

It is not true that the surprise Military Revolution was necessary to save a dying society. For the sick nation, the range of constitutional remedies had not been exhausted. During their last two years in power the military dictators have provided no evidence that they value or intend to restore a free society. They have not talked about freedom. While they have stated that their goal is the establishment of a "genuine democratic republic," they have admitted, curiously, that they do not know what its "political structure" will be like.

The junta's contempt for freedom is demonstrated by the complete destruction of civil liberties. To criticize the junta is a crime. The military dictators are on an anti-Communist crusade carried out by Communist methods. The result could eventually be a popular uprising which could easily be captured by the Communists and used for their purposes. Whatever happens in the future, the Communists no doubt are gloating. Trouble anywhere in the free world is a psychological boon for the Red Conspiracy. In South Korea, where America has expended so much blood and money to preserve liberty and self-rule, it poses particularly attractive possibilities for Red exploitation.

In the present situation the United States should insist upon the sovereign right of the Korean people to decide the kind of society and form of government under which they wish to live. The Korean people cannot exercise this right under a military-police dictatorship. Therefore, the military rulers should restore the Constitution of the Republic of Korea, resign their commissions and submit themselves and their policies to the Korean people in a free general election.

Korea's military rulers are gambling that the United States will support any regime in Korea which is anti-Communist. Unless constitutional democracy is promptly restored in Korea, the United States ought to withdraw completely its economic and military support. Because of American strong identification with Korea, a totalitarian dictatorship of the right is just as damaging to America's international position as a totalitarian dictatorship of the left.

Graduate Student In Government
Woo Jung Ju
From Korea

✿ ✿ ✿

40

LETTERS TO EDITOR—

On South Korean Politics...

Dear Editor,

Day by day, the South Korean military junta looks more and more like the Syngman Rhee regime in its final days. The American stake in South Korea is still high. Not only the Koreans but all Asians are watching the American performance.

Unfortunately, South Korea has become a paradise for opportunists who believe that the loudest protestations of anti-communism are a foolproof method of obtaining American arms and dollars to maintain themselves in power. They charge anyone, whom they dislike, as being pro-communist, including the deposed Roman Catholic Prime Minister, John M. Chang.

At the outset, the junta put a straightjacket on the press. If any publisher wanted to stay in business, he had to "hear no evil, see no evil and speak no evil." Several publications were shut down, a newspaper publisher was executed and a number of editors and reporters were imprisoned.

Finally, Gen. Chang Hee Park, Chairman of the Supreme Council for National Reconstruction (junta), placed a big sword over the press last June 28 by laying down a "press policy." Here are a few interesting points of his edict:

"The Public Information Ministry will judge the qualifications of newspaper publishers, will establish the standards of the newspaper business and will encourage voluntary closedown of disqualified newspapers. The government will not enforce purification of the press but it expects self-purification as promised previously by the representatives of the publishers and editors. . . ."

To "Amend" the constitution "Democratically," the junta held a "referendum" last December. In reality, it was a dictum, because no debate was allowed on the subject. This new constitution grants the president wide power. He can appoint his cabinet members, including the prime minister, without the consent of the National Assembly (unicameral.)

The scandals included an alleged $23 million manipulation of the stock market and profiting from last summer's currency conversion, from government-financed construction and from motor imports from Japan.

On February 18, Gen. Park had been forced to announce the postponement of the election to sometime before August 15. He also offered to renounce his intention of running for the presidency if all political parties and elements pledged to support his nine-point proposal, the most important points of which are: the armed forces to maintain political neutrality; the future civil government to carry out the objectives of the 1960 student revolt and the 1961 military coup.

On February 27, 6 political leaders signed a document promising to uphold these conditions and the chief of the armed services pledged that the military would remain politically neutral.

After declaring his formal withdrawal from the presidential race, Gen. Park confessed that his regime had "completely failed to achieve the objective of regenerating Korean politicals and reconstructing the national character." He also announced the removal of 2322 names from the political black list. Momentarily, this dramatic performance relieved much of the nation's anxiety.

While these pledges and declarations were still ringing in Korea ears, Gen. Park turned the whole affair into a farce with one bold stroke. On March 16 he announced a four-year extension of his rule, nullifying the promised elections for restoring civil government.

Under heavy pressure, Park wavered again. On March 19, he withdrew his proposal for reconsideration and reportedly indicated that he might abandon it if "tainted, corrupt" politicians would refrain from returning to politics.

Park is undoubtedly a power-hungry man, but he is also a man of fear. In February of this year, he agreed to quit politics because he was afraid the army was unreliable. Next, he arrested en masse his former comrades-in-arms, because he was afraid of them, too. Now, he wants to remain in power at any cost, because, among other things, he is afraid he will be retaliated against when he leaves the government. Of Park's original colleagues, numbering over thirty, only three are left now. Hated by the people, unsure of the rank and file military support, the Park dictatorship is wholly unstable and unreliable.

Park accepted the presidential nomination of the Junta party. Park now is taking an entirely different course from its original pledge: "As soldiers, after we have completed our mission we shall restore the government to honest and consientious civilians and return to our military duties."

Power hungry Gen. Park must resign his presidential candidate and establish an interim caretaker government "most qualified to guarantee free elections."

All Koreans must remember that when a government becomes destructive to the good of the people, it is our right, it is our duty — as we demonstrated in the April 1960 Revolution — to institute a new government for the security and welfare of the people.

Woo Jung J
Graduate Student in Government
from Kor

DEPARTMENT OF STATE

Washington, D.C. 20520

August 25, 1969

Woo Jung Ju, Ph.D.
Professor of History
Texas College
Tyler, Texas

Dear Professor Ju:

I have been asked to reply to your letter of
August 11 to President Nixon in which you called
upon the President to cancel his meeting,
scheduled for August 21, with President Park
Chung Hee of the Republic of Korea.

The meeting with President Park, which was
arranged some months ago, was one of many which
President Nixon has had with heads of friendly
states to discuss matters of concern to both
countries. As to question of the United States
view of the proposed amendment to the Republic
of Korea constitution which would permit President
Park to serve a third term, it is the United
States position that this is an internal Korean
matter and the U.S. position is one of impartiality
and non-involvement.

Sincerely yours,

Henry Bardach
Country Officer for Korea

42

The Virginian-Pilot

ESTABLISHED NOVEMBER 21, 1865

Page A16 L   Thursday, November 7, 1974

Norfolk, Portsmouth, Virginia Beach, Chesapeake, and Suffolk, Virginia

Letters to the Editor

Tyranny in South Korea

Editor, Virginian-Pilot:

Park Chung Hee's fascist military government in South Korea has become an outrageously tyrannical, totalitarian, and autocratic regime backed by American tanks, guns, dollars, and bread, and an expensive bodyguard of 40,000 American soldiers. In Park's recent ruthless repression, many thousand South Koreans—chiefly students, professors, and clergymen—have been arrested for political crimes, tried before the military courts, and denied witnesses in their behalf.

The most effective deterrent to Communist gains has proved to be the anti-Communist regime dedicated to solving its nation's problems and able to hold the loyalty of its own people. The Park government had failed to gain or retain the South Korean people's recognition as popular, effective nationalists. Incompetence and corruption have sown the seeds of serious advances of Communism.

Under Syngman Rhee corruption was covert and restrained by the barriers of practicality and good form; it is now unlimited, all-pervasive, and naked of hypocrisy. To the end of helping the Park regime, American officials not only have concealed the corruption and the destruction of basic human rights by the government but have suppressed information about extortion rackets, pillage, and outright Korean CIA atrocities. The main efforts of the United States in Korea have been destructive rather than constructive.

Park's regime is corrupt, inefficient, and unjust because the Americans want it that way. Park's military junta deposed Dr. John M. Chang's seven-month-old parliamentary government, the first democratic government in Korean history, in 1961 while 50,000 American soldiers and officials slept. At that time the United States did not protect even Prime Minister Chang's personal safety.

President Ford is bowing to expediency in pursuing partnership with military dictator Park. Mr. Ford's trip to South Korea reaffirms Park's ruthless, repressive policies and the grave risks for the South Korean people. I hope President Ford cancels his trip to South Korea. If he lacks the power to change it for the better, he should wash America's hands of South Korea.

WOO JUNG JU, Ph.D.,
Professor of History,
Elizabeth City State University.
Elizabeth City.

43

January 6, 1975

Dr. Woo Jung Ju
Elizabeth City State University
Elizabeth City, North Carolina 27909

Dear Dr. Ju:

President Ford has asked me to reply to your comments on political trends
in the Republic of Korea. We are pleased that you have given us the benefit
of your thinking.

In early 1974 the Korean Government issued three emergency decrees pro-
scribing certain forms of political activity which the government considered detrimental to the country's national security. These measures
made it an offense to advocate revision of changes made in the Korean
Constitution in 1972 and prohibited student political activity. They
also established courts martial to try individuals accused of violating
the emergency measures. Penalties were set at a maximum of fifteen
years' imprisonment, except for certain instances, involving participation in or support for a student group accused of plotting to overthrow
the government, in which the death penalty could be applied. The issu-
ance of these decrees was made possible by the 1972 constitutional changes,
which resulted in a highly centralized and authoritarian form of government
in South Korea.

The two most severe emergency measures--prohibiting support for constitutional revision and student political activity--were lifted in late August.
During the period these two decrees were in effect, approximately 200
persons were tried and sentenced. Most of the cases are being appealed,
and many of the sentences have been reduced by appellate courts. In several instances in which the death penalty was meted out, sentences were
commuted to life imprisonment; in some cases sentences have been suspended.

While we understand your concern, the actions which our government
might appropriately take with respect to the treatment by the Korean Government of its own citizens are understandably limited.

We also understand your concern about the presence of American
troops in Korea and US aid to the South Korean Government. American military forces are not stationed in Korea or anywhere else to support a particular government. They are stationed abroad when necessary to enhance
our own security, to deter aggression, or when their presence serves to
prevent instability in an area of tension. Similarly, American assistance
programs are intended to support the economic development of the Republic
of Korea and to contribute to development of a situation of stability on
the Korean peninsula.

The North Korean regime continues to manifest its aggressive designs on South Korea, and the threat of large-scale North Korean aggression remains real. US aid seeks to deter such aggression by enhancing South Korea's security and by providing visible evidence of our continued commitment to that country. As such, it is an important element in our efforts to assure the stability and security of Northeast Asia, a region where Soviet, Chinese, and US interests converge. In our view, the prevention of war on the Korean peninsula is in itself a moral consideration of overwhelming importance.

I am pleased to enclose for you a Department of State report which describes our concern about the problem of human rights in Korea and explains our policies there.

Sincerely,

Carol C. Laise
Assistant Secretary
for Public Affairs

Enclosure.

Letters to the Editor

Overlong in South Korea

Editor, Virginian-Pilot:

The United States should withdraw its 40,000 troops from South Korea. Park Chung Hee's fascist military government has become an outrageously tyrannical, totalitarian, and autocratic regime backed by American tanks, guns, dollars, bread, and an expensive bodyguard of American soldiers.

Koreans believe that self-determination and preservation should be respected and that we should be allowed to handle our own domestic and military affairs without intervention from outside powers. The United States prevented the Communist armed aggression of 1950 and has given South Koreans time to achieve economic, military, and political stability.

South Korea maintains 600,000 regular troops who have received advanced military training from American military advisers since 1950 and are capable of defending their own country. Meanwhile, American military personnel and excess Korean soldiers in South Korea are deeply involved in Korean political activities. Their influence not only jeopardizes democracy, but also contaminates the stability of democratic institutions. Koreans are baffled by U.S. backing of the Park Chung Hee clique. Nationalism is on the march in Korea as elsewhere, and the United States can ignore it only at its own risk.

Park Chung Hee's government is corrupt, inefficient, and unjust because the Americans want it that way. Democratic intellectuals and church leaders have been arrested, tortured, and killed because they sought minimum human rights from the Park Chung Hee clique. The Park Government is becoming like the North Korean Government.

Park's military junta deposed Dr. John M. Chang's seven-month-old parliamentary government, the first democratic government in Korean history, in 1961 while 50,000 American soldiers and officials slept. At that time the United States did not guard even Prime Minister Chang's personal safety. The United States is bowing to expediency in pursuing partnership with military dictator Park Chung Hee and reaffirming Park's ruthless, repressive policies.

Joining with our conscientious countrymen everywhere I earnestly urge the United States to withdraw its troops from South Korea at once to redress the wrongs inflicted upon the South Korean people, and in so doing restore the honor of the South Korean nation.

WOO JUNG IU, Ph.D.
Professor of History,
Elizabeth City State University.
Elizabeth City, N.C.

Page A16

The Virginian-Pilot

ESTABLISHED NOVEMBER 21, 1865

Wednesday, September 1, 1976

Norfolk, Portsmouth, Virginia Beach, Chesapeake, and Suffolk, Virginia

Human Rights in South Korea

Editor, Virginian-Pilot:

We hailed President Carter's proclaimed intention to speak out against human-rights violations anywhere in the world. We applauded President Carter's denunciation of the Kremlin's persecution of Soviet dissidents. But what about the violation of human rights by the Park Chung Hee government in South Korea?

President Carter has heard appalling reports about what has been happening to individual freedom under the Park Chung Hee regime—torture, political arrests, trumped-up charges, bogus trials followed quickly by executions, detention without trial, closing of universities, press censorship, loss of employment by dissenters, heavy police surveillance, and a national legislature that mocks representative government. U.S. policymakers are fully aware that the atmosphere of police surveillance in South Korea is heavy.

What of President Carter's human-rights promise? What is the difference between white Russians and yellow Koreans? Mr. Carter's attention is desperately needed by the Korean people because Park Chung Hee's outrageously tyrannical regime is backed by American tanks, guns, dollars, bread, and an expensive bodyguard of 30,-000 American soldiers. Mr. Carter is bowing to expediency in pursuing partnership with dictator Park Chung Hee and reaffirming his repressive policies.

Violation of elementary human rights by the Park Chung Hee regime is escalating. Democratic intellectuals and church leaders have been arrested, tortured, and killed because they sought minimum human rights from the Park Chung Hee government.

We have yet to hear Mr. Carter speak in behalf of these Korean dissidents. On the contrary, he expressed willingness to receive Park Chung Hee, a terrible violator of human rights and a traitor who belonged to the Japanese Imperial special military duty officer corps that destroyed and assassinated Korean patriots and anti-Japanese exiles in Manchuria during World War II.

Mr. Carter is under the influence of selfish interest groups that represent not the American people but multinational corporations. These powerful groups mistakenly regarded Park Chung Hee as the protector of U.S. interests. They are also arguing in favor of Park Chung Hee under the illusion that both U.S. and Japanese interests are identical for all the time. President Theodore Roosevelt and William H. Taft thought so, and turned Korea over to Japan in 1910. Japan used Korea as a stepping stone for conquest of all Asia and attacked on Pearl Harbor in 1941.

Getting rid of the Park Chung Hee government is more urgent than maintenance of U.S. troops in South Korea. Batista brought Castro in Cuba, Chiang Kai-shek caused Mao Tse-tung's revolution in China. Diem and Thieu fetched the Vietcong in Vietnam. Nicaraguans are rebelling against President Somoza's dictatorship. Park Chung Hee will be the next to invite revolt.

WOO JUNG JU, Ph.D.
Professor of History,
Elizabeth City State University.
Elizabeth City, N.C.

47

Carter keeps silent
on Korean abuses

Thursday, February 8, 1979 — The Daily Advance — Forum — Elizabeth City, N.C. 27909

To the Editor:

The Iranian revolution has not yet ended. No matter which way it goes and how it will ultimately affect the people of Iran, it is already shaping up as a sure plus for the Soviet Union and a big minus for the United States. U.S. approved military dictator Park Chung Hee in South Korea will be the next to invite revolt and bring a second South Vietnam or a second Iran.

Korean people hailed President Carter's proclaimed intention to speak out against human-rights violations anywhere in the world. We applauded President Carter's denunciation of the Kremlin's persecution of Soviet dissidents. But what about the violation of human rights by the Park Chung Hee government in South Korea?

President Carter has heard appalling reports about what has been happening to individual freedom under the Park Chung Hee regime — torture, political arrests, trumped-up charges, bogus trials followed quickly by executions, detention without trial, press censorship, heavy police surveillance and a national legislature that mocks representative government. United States policymakers are fully aware that the atmosphere of police surveillance in South Korea is heavy.

Methods of torture by the Park Chung Hee regime include whipping with wires, the beating of the soles of the feet, kicking, burning of parts of the body with cigarettes, extended sleep deprivation combined with forced standing, the application of nettles to sensitive parts of the body and long periods of solitary confinement.

What of President Carter's human-rights promise? With his concern for human rights, why does President Carter's support for Park Chung Hee continue untempered? Why has President Carter kept his silence on human rights abuses by the Park Chung Hee government? Mr. Carter's attention is desperately needed by the Korean people because Park Chung Hee's outrageously tyrannical regime is backed by American tanks, guns, dollars, bread and an expensive bodyguard of 30,000 American soldiers. Mr. Carter is bowing to expediency in pursuing partnership with dictator Park Chung Hee and reaffirming his repressive policies.

We have yet to hear Mr. Carter speak in behalf of these Korean dissidents. On the contrary, he expressed willingness to meet Park Chung Hee in the summer of 1979 in Seoul. Park Chung Hee is a terrible violator of human rights and a traitor who belonged to the Japanese Imperial Special military duty corps that destroyed and assassinated Korean patriots and anti-Japanese exiles in Manchuria during the Second World War. When we see the South Korean dictator Park Chung Hee and President Carter together in Seoul, President Carter's credibility on human rights will die away electronically. President Carter's visit to fascist military dictator Park Chung Hee would serve only to strengthen a tyrannical and autocratic Park Chung Hee regime.

Getting rid of the Park Chung Hee government is more urgent than maintenance of U.S. troops in South Korea and is the only way to the restoration of human rights and to bring liberty, justice, peace, security and national strength. We knew well that Batista brought Castro in Cuba, Chiang Kai-shek caused Mao Tse-tung's revolution in China, Diem and Thieu fetched the Vietcong in Vietnam. The Shah of Iran has sown the seeds of unpredictable revolution and went into exile. Park Chung Hee will be the next to bring another disastrous setback for the United States.

The breakdown of the European colonial powers after the Second World War followed the turmoil of national liberation, coups d'etats, and civil wars. The United States has allowed itself to be aligned with the status quo which has no popular support.

Why did American foreign policy commit itself to supporting a reactionary regime, which advocates anti-Communist policies to sustain their power with American aids? The turmoils after the Second World War will continue for decades, perhaps for generations. If the United States continues to maintain status quo, she is likely to go down with face the factor of reactionary governments.

Woo Jung Ju

(Editor's Note: Woo Jung Ju is a native of Bucheun, Korea. He has taught at Ewha Women's University in Seoul, Korea, and at Texas College in Tyler, Texas. Since 1969 he has been a professor of history at Elizabeth City State University.)

United States Senate
WASHINGTON, D.C. 20510

February 13, 1979

Professor Woo Jung Ju
Elizabeth City State Univ.
Elizabeth City, North Carolina 27909

Dear Professor Ju:

Thank you for your views on recent human rights violations.
Please be assured that I share your deep concern over this
serious issue. Obviously, there are many goals on the agenda of
human rights and humanitarian concerns yet to be achieved.
Exerting our influence for political, economic and social rights,
submitting for ratification many of the human rights covenants
which have been gathering dust for so many years, revising our
immigration laws to make us once more the citadel of hope for
political refugees from repression of the left to the right,
ensuring that our aid does not help dictatorial regimes remain in
power -- these are all important priorities.

I will continue to strongly advocate and support effective
rights policies as a critical element in our relations with other
countries. During future consideration of this issue by the
Senate, your views and comments will continue to have my most
careful attention.

Again, thank you for writing.

Sincerely,

Edward M. Kennedy

FRANK CHURCH, IDAHO CHAIRMAN

CLAIBORNE PELL, R.I.   JACOB K. JAVITS, N.Y.
GEORGE MC GOVERN, S. DAK.   CHARLES H. PERCY, ILL.
JOSEPH R. BIDEN, JR., DEL.   HOWARD H. BAKER, JR., TENN.
JOHN GLENN, OHIO   JESSE HELMS, N.C.
RICHARD (DICK) STONE, FLA.   S. I. HAYAKAWA, CALIF.
PAUL S. SARBANES, MD.   RICHARD G. LUGAR, IND.
EDMUND MUSKIE, MAINE
EDWARD ZORINSKY, NEBR.

WILLIAM B. BADER, STAFF DIRECTOR

United States Senate

COMMITTEE ON FOREIGN RELATIONS
WASHINGTON, D.C. 20510

March 13, 1979

Woo Jung Ju, Ph. D.
Department of History
Elizabeth City State University
Elizabeth City, North Carolina 27909

Dear Dr. Ju:

Thank you for your letter regarding the violations of human rights in the Republic of Korea. Certainly, the combination of Emergency Degree #9, forbidding any criticism of the government, the centralized power of the Yushin Constitution, and the allegations of torture are profoundly disturbing. Dissidents remain in jail. However, I am encouraged by the recent release of Kim Dae Jung and other political prisoners. These releases, I believe, stem in part from the international pressure generated against the repression in South Korea.

The Committee on Foreign Relations is monitoring this situation carefully and will consider the record of the South Korean Government in evaluating military assistance requests this year.

I appreciate your taking the time to write and give me your views.

With best wishes,

Sincerely,

Frank Church
Chairman

The Washington Post

WEDNESDAY, JUNE 13, 1979

Seoul's Welcome for Carter

A letter in the June 5 Washington Post from Woo Jung Ju, a professor at Elizabeth City State University, subjects your readers to distortions of facts and to unwarranted slurs on my country and its government.

Professor Woo gives a most inaccurate portrayal of civic conditions in the Republic of Korea. He attacks our Constitution, which has been overwhelmingly approved by the Korean electorate. He misinforms your readers by such statements that my government "is destroying Christian organizations and foreign missionaries in South Korea." There is, in fact, complete freedom of religion, including freedom to proselytize in South Korea. Almost 5 million Korean Christians support dozens of thriving church-related institutions of higher learning—many with American ties. As our minister of foreign affairs told a New York audience early this year, "Perhaps nowhere else in Asia will you find a deeper and stronger feeling of spiritual fellowship and psychological affinity toward the American experience and toward Americans than you will in Korea."

On the other hand, the professor completely ignores the military threat from the North (where all religious practice is proscribed). This threat, however, is a major concern to all of us. He also says nothing of the great improvement in the quality of life in Korea and of the fair sharing of the fruits of our progress—an equity unsurpassed in Asia, or for that matter, in most parts of the world.

A need for a mutual and realistic assessment of the security situation and of the burgeoning trade between our two nations forms the basis for the close consultations between the two governments. Such sessions have been traditional in U.S.-Korean relations for 30 years. The people of the Republic of Korea will welcome President Carter not for any short-term benefits—as Professor Woo charges—but out of enduring respect and friendship for America and Americans.

SU-DOC KIM,
Director, Office of Information,
Embassy of Korea.

Washington

51

June 22, 1979

Professor Woo Jung Ju
Department of History
Elizabeth City State University
Elizabeth City, North Carolina 27909

Dear Professor Ju:

I am replying to your message to President Carter regarding his meeting with President Park Chung Hee of the Republic of Korea.

President Carter has accepted President Park's invitation to visit Seoul immediately after the conference of industrialized nations in Tokyo in late June. Although the many issues which arise between our two nations are the subject of regular consultation between officials, there are certain important matters of vital mutual interest between close allies and economic partners which properly engage the involvement of the leaders of both countries. It is therefore normal and important that the two Presidents from time to time meet personally to ensure the orderly handling of such issues and to improve mutual understanding at all levels. Before the meeting is held, all major issues, including human rights, will be carefully reviewed for consideration by the two presidents.

On numerous occasions, the U.S. Government has made clear to the Korean Government at all levels our concern about infringements of the right to peaceful protest and expression of one's views. We have pointed out the concern that many Americans feel over such limitations and have noted the unfortunate effects they can have at home and abroad. We will continue to utilize every opportunity effectively to encourage the Korean Government to ease restriction on freedom of expression. As we pursue these efforts, we also try to maintain as accurate a picture as possible of the Korean human rights situation through

contacts with people from all segments of Korean society.
We will continue to accord high priority to human rights
in our dialogue with the Korean Government.

Sincerely,

Hodding Carter III
Assistant Secretary
for Public Affairs and
Department Spokesman

The Daily Advance

Forum

Sunday, July 1, 1979   ELIZABETH CITY, N.C., 27909

Carter's visit to Seoul is disturbing to reader

To the Editor:

We are deeply disturbed when a friend of human rights, President Jimmy Carter, arrived in Seoul from the Tokyo economic summit Friday on June 29 to shake hands with Park Chung Hee, a terrible human rights violator. There is no reason for the American president to visit dictator Park Chung Hee. President Carter and the American public should know the nature of Park and his regime.

Park's Yushin Constitution placed virtually all power in his hands, and permits President Park lifetime tenure, sure control of all branches of the government, and the privilege of governing by decree. Park is the Chairman of the National Conference for Unification, which elects him; and he appoints the members of the Central Election Committee, which oversees elections.

Park appoints one third of the National Assembly and he can' dissolve the National Assembly at any time. Park has the power to appoint and discipline all judge. Park appoints all the members of the constitutional committee that determines whether the laws passed by the National Assembly are constitutional. Should these arrangements be deemed inadequate by Park Chung Hee, he can take emergency measures regarding any of the nation's affairs, whenever, in his judgment, the national security or the public safety and order is seriously threatened or anticipated to be threatened.

Park's Emergency Decree No. 9 provided those who violate this measure are punished by imprisonment of one year to death. Under this Emergency Decree No. 9,

he can jail anyone who criticizes the government, even in private. Democratic intellectuals and church leaders involved in the human-rights movement in South Korea have been tortured, imprisoned, kidnaped and killed by the Park's CIA.

Park Chung Hee is a traitor who belonged to the Japanese Imperial Special Military Duty Corps that destroyed and assassinated Korean patriots and anti-Japanese exiles in Manchuria during the Second World War.

Park Chung Hee was a communist. In 1948 Park had been sentenced to death for his role in a Communist rebellion in Southern South Korea as an army officer. His brother was executed and Park escaped death only by the intervention of U.S. officer.

Park's regime is destroying Christian organizations and foreign Missionaries in South Korea. During last March and April, 15 persons connected with Korean Christian Academy, including 6 staff members, were being held by Park's CIA without informing their families of anything.

South Koreans are under martial law and the rigid control of the KCIA and the secret police. No one is allowed to voice any criticism of the government, the Yushin system or Emergency Decree No.9. People see Park's Korea becoming more and more like North Korea politically.

The massive amount of United States aid to Korea, and particularly the military aid, is repugnant to both American people, whose tax dollars go the support a corrupt dictatorship, and to the South Korean people who suffer under the tyranny of a regime which is maintained by U.S. aid in the

absence of popular support.

It would be unconscionable to visit South Korea at a time when international demands for the immediate and unconditional release of all political prisoners go unheeded.

In Seoul, tens of thousands will turn out to welcome President Carter, and full photos of President Carter and dictator Park embracing would fill newspapers. The propaganda would serve as an indication of official approval of Park's Korea, which is totally lacking in democratic spirit, principles and practices. This would result in the United States government's strengthening Park's hand against the Korean democratic movement. President Carter's visit to Park Chung Hee makes a mockery of his pledge to make human rights a cornerstone of U.S foreign policy.

Woo Jung Ju, Ph.D.
Professor of History
Elizabeth City State Univ.

54

the
Daily Advance

ELIZABETH CITY, N.C., 27909.

, WEDNESDAY, SEPT. 12, 1979

Korean dictator
deserves no support

To the Editor:

It was certain that the Carter-Park summit (earlier this year) was a mistake. In Seoul, full photos of President Carter and dictator Park embracing filled newspapers and the propaganda served to legitimize Park's regime and oppression. In the United States, the summit helped to mold U.S. public opinion toward further military and economic aid to tyrannical, totalitarian and autocratic Park's regime.

U.S. approved military dictator Park Chung Hee will be the next to invite revolt...The United States must speak out against human-rights violations in South Korea. The oppressive and autocratic anti-Communist regimes have sown the seeds of revolutions.

The severest human-rights violations and tortures in South Korea follows the Carter-Park summit. A surprise attack at 2 a.m. Sunday, August 12, 1979 by 1,000 riot police on the headquarters of South Korea's main opposition, New Democratic Party, brought with one death, 100 injured and 198 arrested, according to the New York Times News Service. The riot police also gave a fierce beating to party officials, reporters and senior politicians in the building. Miss Kim Kyung Sook, 21, a textile worker died from a blow on the head and Rep. Kim Hyong Kwang, Rep. Park Kwon Hum and Rep. Kim Chang Ki were hospitalized with internal injuries received and had been hit with bricks in the raid.

On July 23, 1979, Moon-Bu-sik, a former assemblyman and editor of the Democratic Front (the New Democratic Party's main literature), and on August 10, 1979, Chung Kyung-

ho, a Catholic priest, Oh Won-Choon and Chung Jae-don, both members of the Catholic Farmer's Association, were jailed for the alleged violation of Emergency Decree No. 9.

Park's regime is destroying Christian organizations and foreign missionaries in South Korea. During last March 15, persons connected with the Korean Christian Academy, including six staff members, were being held by Park's CIA without informing their families or anything. According to the New York Times News Service, Aug. 26, 1979, the Christian Academy case suggested that the government uses severe tortures to obtain confessions from suspected communist sympathizers. A reporter obtained the statements at a meeting with wives of three of the accused, Lee Woo-jae, Whang Ha-shik and Kim Sae-guyn. The meeting was arranged by the Korea National Council of Churches in Seoul. They agreed to sign statements implicating themselves as Communist sympathizers after many weeks of severe tortures.

Methods of torture by the Park Chung Hee regime include whipping with wires, the beating of the soles of the feet, kicking, burning of parts of the body with cigarettes, extended sleep deprivation combined with forced standing, the application of nettles to sensitive parts of the body and long periods of solitary confinement.

What of President Carter's human rights promise? With his concern for human rights, why does President Carter's support for Park Chung Hee continue untempered? Why has President Carter kept his silence on human rights abuses by the Park Chung Hee regime?

Mr. Carter's attention is desperately needed by the Korean people because Park Chung Hee's outrageously tyrannical regime is backed by American tanks, guns, dollars, bread and (an) expensive bodyguard of 30,000 American soldiers. Mr. Carter is bowing to expediency in pursuing partnership with dictator Park Chung Hee and reaffirming his repressive policies. The Carter-Park summit served only to strengthen a tyrannical and autocratic Park regime and President Carter's Korean policy does not differ from his predecessors' at all.

Woo Jung Ju
Professor of History
ECSU

AGAINST THE TYRANNICAL REGIME OF CHUN DOO HWAN

The Virginian-Pilot

Editorials

Norfolk, Portsmouth, Virginia Beach, Chesapeake, Suffolk

Saturday, August 27, 1983   118th Year, No. 239

The next to go Communist?

Editor, Virginian-Pilot:,

Under no circumstances should President Reagan meet with South Korean President Chun Doo Hwan and Philippine President Ferdinand Marcos as scheduled next fall in Seoul and Manila respectively. There is no good reason for the U.S. president to visit these dictators — only bad ones.

Getting rid of the governments of Chun and Marcos is more urgent than maintenance of U.S. troops in South Korea and the Philippines. American support of dictatorships frequently works against U.S. interests. Batista, who was backed by the United States, paved the way for the triumph of the Castro revolution in Cuba. The corruption of the Chiang Kai-shek regime, also backed by the United States, aided Mao's revolution in China. Diem and Thieu fetched the Vietcong in Vietnam. The Shah of Iran led to the Ayatollah Khomeini's revolution in Iran, which

is now openly anti-American. The Somoza dictatorship resulted in the anti-American Sandinista regime in Nicaragua. El Salvadorans are rebelling against their absolutist government, which the U.S. also supports. Chun Doo Whan and Ferdinand Marcos will be the next to invite Communist revolution.

Mr. Reagan's attention is desperately needed by the Korean and Philippine peoples because the outrageously tyrannical regimes of Chun and Marcos are backed by the American government. Mr. Reagan would be bowing to expediency to mix warmly with dictators Chun and Marcos and, by implication, reaffirm their repressive policies.

Both Korean and Filipino disappointment and frustration have exploded in the burning of the U.S. cultural centers and flags and in expressions of anti-Americanism on campuses and in the streets. Any gains for the United States

from the scheduled summit meeting would be greatly outweighed by U.S. embarrassments and concessions and Philippine and South Korean exploitation, the prestige of President Reagan.

In Seoul and Manila, full photos President Reagan and dictators Chun an Marcos embracing would fill newspaper The propaganda would serve to legi mize the oppression of the Chun and Ma cos regimes. The U.S. summit would he to mold U.S. public opinion toward fu ther military and economic aid to Ch Doo Hwan and Ferdinand Marcos.

President Reagan's visit to dictatc Chun and Marcos would serve only strengthen the hand of Chun and Marc against the democratic forces worki for human rights in South Korea and t Philippines. Such summit meetings this time would be inappropriate a should be canceled immediately,

WOO JUNG J

Virginia Beach.

CHARLES H. PERCY, ILL., CHAIRMAN

OWARD H. BAKER, JR., TENN.   CLAIBORNE PELL, R.I.
SSE HELMS, N.C.   JOSEPH R. BIDEN, JR., DEL.
CHARD G. LUGAR, IND.   JOHN GLENN, OHIO
ARLES McC. MATHIAS, JR., MD.   PAUL S. SARBANES, MD.
NCY L. KASSEBAUM, KANS.   EDWARD ZORINSKY, NEBR.
OY BOSCHWITZ, MINN.   PAUL E. TSONGAS, MASS.
RRY PRESSLER, S. DAK.   ALAN CRANSTON, CALIF.
ANK H. MURKOWSKI, ALASKA   CHRISTOPHER J. DODD, CONN.

        SCOTT COHEN, STAFF DIRECTOR
GERYLD B. CHRISTIANSON, MINORITY STAFF DIRECTOR

United States Senate

COMMITTEE ON FOREIGN RELATIONS

WASHINGTON, D.C. 20510

November 1, 1983

Professor Woo Jung Ju
Department of History
Elizabeth City State University
Elizabeth City, North Carolina 27909

Dear Professor Ju:

Thank you for your recent letter. I understand your view,
but I have not opposed the President's trip to Korea. The
Korean people have suffered two traumatic events in recent
weeks: the downing of the Korean airliner by the Soviet Union
and the assassination in Rangoon of seventeen top Korean
officials. President Reagan will be offering American
condolences in person as well as reaffirming the U.S.
security commitment to Korea. I cannot think of a more
appropriate time for a Presidential visit to that country.

I agree with your view that the United States must continue
to support political liberalization in Korea and must
convince the current government that Korean security will be
enhanced by improved individual and press freedom. I have
made that point myself on a number of occasions. I am
sending you a copy of a speech I made on U.S.-Korean
relations some time ago, in case you might be interested in
reading it.

Sincerely,

Charles H. Percy
Chairman

CHP:awm

Enclosure

United Movement for Democracy and Unification in Korea

P.O. Box 3657   Arlington, Virginia 22203   (202) 265-9808

NEWS RELEASE

May 19 Demonstration will Picket
Heritage Foundation on Anniversary of Massacre

Contact:
Rev. Stephen Tonghwan Moon
202-265-9808
or
Marc J. Cohen
202-547-6406

May 15, 1984

Washington, DC -- Several US-based Korean organizations, along with church groups and human rights organizations, will demonstrate on May 19 against a Visiting Fellow at the Heritage Foundation whom they charge shares responsibility for the death of two thousand people in South Korea.

According to spokesperson the Reverend Stephen Tonghwan Moon, the groups are concerned that the Foundation, a conservative "think tank", has given a Visiting Fellowship at its Asian Studies Center to General Hur Hwa Pyung, a retired South Korean Army officer.

Moon, Chairperson of the United Movement for Democracy and Unification in Korea (UMDUK), says, "It is unconscionable for the Heritage Foundation to provide haven for a figure associated with massive abuse of human rights."

According to Moon, who is a political exile from South Korea, Gen. Hur shares responsibility with current South Korean President Chun Doo Hwan for the deaths of 2,000 people in Kwangju, South Korea four years ago. In addition, Moon says, "During the period of martial law in South Korea in 1980, Hur had responsibilit for the interrogation, which often included torture, of the leaders of the democratic movement.

Moon also emphasizes that Koreans widely believe

that Gen. Hur insisted that the military government ex-

ecute Kim Dae Jung, the opposition leader who currently

lives in exile in the United States.

Moon explains that in 1980, following the assassinat

of General Park Chung-hee, the South Korean military rule

from 1961 to 1979, large-scale demonstrations favoring the restoration of democracy occurred in South Cholla Province, a region of four million people, of which Kwangju is the capital.

Chun, who was then Defense Security Commander, sent troops to suppress the protest, Moon asserts. At least 2,000 people were killed between May 18 and 27, 1980. At that time, Moon adds, Hur was Chun's chief of staff, "and was therefore a key figure in the chain of command which ordered the brutal repression at Kwangju."

Moon says the coalition of groups opposed to Hur's presence in the United States will stage a demonstration in Washington, DC, on May 19, 1984. At 3:00 p.m., a ceremony honoring the dead of Kwangju will be held at the park across the street from Union Station, at First and D Streets, N.E.

Following the memorial gathering, Moon says that the protestors, "who will include Americans, Koreans,and... Third World people living in the United States," will procede to the Heritage Foundation at Second and Massachusetts Avenue, N.E. A picket line will be formed, demanding the cancellation of Hur's fellowship and his deportation.

Moon says the demonstrators will then proceed to the White House for a vigil to protest the Reagan Administration's support for military rule in South Korea. At the

White House, the group will hear a message from Kim Dae Jung.

According to Moon, while picketing the Heritage Foundation, the protestors will stage "guerrilla theater skits, aimed at exposing the torture techniques that the South Korean government employed in 1980, and continues to use to harrass and intimidate popular demands for democracy."

Moon adds that several victims of torture in South Korea will attend the demonstration and will speak to the pickets. For example, Lee Shin-Bom, Director of the Commission on U.S.-Asian Relations and former Secretary of the Amnesty International Korean Committee, will be available for interviews.

The organizations sponsering the demonstration, in addition to UMDUK, include the Committee for the Memorial Service for the Kwangju Massacre; the North American Coalition for Human Rights in Korea, which is sponsored by a number of American churches; and the Commission on U.S.-Asian Relations, a project of the Center for Development Policy. UMDUK is an association of Korean residents of the United States and Canada which strives to promote democracy in South Korea. Its members are engaged in business, professional, religious, and academic occupations.

RICHARD G. LUGAR, INDIANA, CHAIRMAN

JESSE HELMS, NORTH CAROLINA   CLAIRORNE PELL, RHODE ISLAND
CHARLES McC. MATHIAS, JR., MARYLAND   JOSEPH H. BIDEN, JR., DELAWARE
NANCY L. KASSEBAUM, KANSAS   PAUL S. SARBANES, MARYLAND
RUDY BOSCHWITZ, MINNESOTA   EDWARD ZORINSKY, NEBRASKA
LARRY PRESSLER, SOUTH DAKOTA   ALAN CRANSTON, CALIFORNIA
FRANK H. MURKOWSKI, ALASKA   CHRISTOPHER J. DODD, CONNECTICUT
PAUL S. TRIBLE, JR., VIRGINIA   THOMAS F. EAGLETON, MISSOURI
DANIEL J. EVANS, WASHINGTON   JOHN F. KERRY, MASSACHUSETTS

M. GRAEME BANNERMAN, STAFF DIRECTOR
GERYLD B. CHRISTIANSON, MINORITY STAFF DIRECTOR

United States Senate

COMMITTEE ON FOREIGN RELATIONS

WASHINGTON, DC 20510

August 1, 1986

Woo Jung Ju, Ph.D.
Professor of History
Elizabeth City State University
Elizabeth City, North Carolina 27909

Dear Professor Ju:

Thank you for your July 9, 1986, correspondence. I
certainly share in your support for democracy in the Republic
of Korea.

The relationship between Korea and the United States is
a very special one. It has been forged in a war to preserve
the independence of Korea and strengthened over the decades
through the diligent efforts of both nations. Korea has
emerged as one of the most dynamic economic powers of Asia.
The United States views Korea as a stable, maturing
democracy, and we wish to reinforce this trend.

The broader question of human rights in Korea, which is
closely related to the establishment of a stable democracy,
is of enduring concern to the Foreign Relations Committee.
Though there has been progress in several areas, there is
room for significant improvement. As Chairman of the
Committee, I can assure you that we will continue to
encourage respect for human rights and a full democracy in
South Korea.

Again, thank you for contacting me.

Sincerely,

Richard G. Lugar
Chairman

RGL:lpj

JOHN W. WARNER
VIRGINIA

ARMED SERVICES COMMITTEE
Chairman, Strategic and Theater Nuclear Force
Subcommittee

ENERGY AND NATURAL RESOURCES COMMITTEE
Chairman, Energy and Mineral Resources
Subcommittee

RULES AND ADMINISTRATION COMMITTEE

JOINT COMMITTEE ON THE LIBRARY OF CON

United States Senate
WASHINGTON, D.C. 20510

September 9, 1986

Dr. Woo Jung Ju
648 Rosaer Lane
Virginia Beach, VA 23464

Dear Dr. Ju:

Thank you for expressing your views concerning the democratic movement in South Korea.

As a veteran of the Korean War, I too am sensitive to the need for more democratic reforms which will help the security of South Korea in the long run. I am hopeful that President Chun Doo Hwan will soon consent to direct Presidential elections and other reforms. While the economic achievements of South Korea since the war have been significant, I believe political reform will help enfranchise more consumers into its economy in addition to bringing more sensitivity to civil rights.

On the other hand, the threat from North Korea has not diminished. Whatever changes occur in South Korea, they must not weaken the country to the extent it cannot deter war with North Korea. Events such as the Rangoon bombing do not increase the South Korean leadership's desire for greater pluralism.

Please accept my sincere apologies for the delayed response. Despite extensive efforts by me and my staff to ensure that all mail is answered promptly and efficiently, we still make some mistakes. And with the thousands of letters I receive weekly, I know you will understand that a letter can occasionally be mishandled or misplaced.

Sincerely,

John W. Warner

JWW/bg

64

SOUTH KOREANS PROTEST—Members of the Korean Committee for Democratic Action picket the White House after demonstrating yesterday before the South Korean Embassy to protest the move by South Korean President Chung Hee Park to amend the country's constitution in order for him to serve a third term.

한 민 신 보

HAN MIN SHIN BO BULK RATE POSTAGE PAID ARLINGTON, VA. PERMIT 17

2732 N. WASHINGTON BLVD. ARLINGTON, VA.

1983년 6월 25일

김대중씨 부부
미국민주당 중진 만찬 참석
주우정 박사가 수행

김대중씨

미국 민주당기금을 위한 만찬회에 김대중씨 부부와 전 한민신보 회장주 우정 박사가 참석하여 시선을 끌었다.

차기 민주당 대통령후보 물망에 올 라있는 「존·글렌」「게리·하트」

「월터·몬데일」「알렌·크랜스턴」「어 스트·홀링스」씨등 상원의원들이 참석한 파티는 지난 14일 버지니아 메클린 소재 에드워드·케네디」의원의 자택에서 열렸 다.

「토마스·오닐」하원 의장과 민주당 의장「로버트·버드」씨의 초청형식으로 최된 이날 파티장에서 김대중씨 부부와 우정 박사는 미정계 요인들과 한국의 화에 대해 광범위한 의견을 교환한 것 알려졌다.

김대중씨는 이자리에서 「엔드루·영 유엔대사와 반가운 해후를 나눈후 잠시 귓속말을 주고받았다고 한 참석자가 전

2백여명이 참석한 이날 저녁 파티 비는 1인당 1천달러 였으며 차기 대 후보로 나설 정치인들은 각각 3분씩의 설시간을 할애받고 유머를 섞어가며 정 발표했다.

전 한민신보 회장 주우정 박사는 「 디」상원의원의 가장 신임받고 있는 한

66

포가운데 한사람으로써 오랫동안 『케네디』 의원을 위한 모금활동, 홍보활동에 종사해 오고있다.

주우정 박사는 버지니아주 『킨 엘리자 베드』 대학교의 국제정치학 교수 로 재직중 이다.

◆ 케네디 상원의원의 한국인 제일측근 으로 알려진 주우정 박사

The Korea -America Times

1983 년 8 월 20 일

문동환 목사 의장에 재선

부의장=김신형, 한완상, 주우정 씨

사무총장 최성일씨 유임

한민통 연차총회 기관지 발행

【워싱턴】민통연합 제2차 정기총회가 지난 13일 상오 9시부터 하오 6시까지 버지니아 스프링필드 근처에 있는 임페리얼 호텔 400에서 개최되었다.

미국과 캐나다 지역에서 대표들 80여명이 참석한 이번 정기총회에서는 총회전 떠돌던 말과는 달리 별다른 새제 변동없이 진행되었다.

최성일 사무총장의 업무보고와 함께 앞으로의 활동방향이 논의되었는데

① 교포 권익과 조국민주화를 위해 조직 강화

② 미국 선거에 적극 참여하여 조국 민주화를 위한 활동 강화를 다짐했다.

또 ③ 워싱턴에 사무실을 차리고 유급 간사를 두어 활동 방향을 강화한다는데 합의했다.

한편 임원 선서에서 들어가 문동환 목사를 다시 의장으로 유임시키고 3명의 부의장을 임명했는데 한완상 부의장은 그대로 유임되었다.

신임 부회장 2명은 서부지역에서 김신형(김상돈씨 따님)씨와 주우정 박사를 임명했다.

사무총장에는 최성일씨가 그대로 유임되었다.

한편 민통연합은 워싱턴에서 기관지인 신문을 발행하기로 의견을 모았다.

상임위원에는 김영삼씨 계열인 임정규, 조응규 씨 등이 새로 영입되었으며 실행위원에는 뉴욕의 임병규씨 등이 새로운 모습을' 보였다.

상임위원과 실행위원 등은 다음과 같다.

▲ 상임위원

임정규, 동원모, 김정순, 김동건, 김경, 김경제, 김응태, 구춘회 김마택, 곽노순, 이학인, 이재현, 이하전, 이근팔, 이상철, 이성호, 이승만, 임병규, 명재휘, 박찬웅, 유시홍, 손명걸, 김광정, 조응교, 장지원, 서유웅 및 각지장 위원장.

▲ 실행위원

문동화, 김신형, 최성일, 이재현, 김응태, 이상철, 임병규.

▲ 감사 : 김윤철, 정의순.

민통연합 간부들 오른 쪽으로 부터 주우정, 한완상 부의장

HAN MIN SHIN BO   BULK. RATE POSTAGE PAID ARLINGTON, VA.
2192 N. WASHINGTON BLVD.

제 245호   1983년 9월 1일

『 민통연합 정기총회 』

교포사회 조직확대보다 대미활동에
주력할듯
문동환 주우정 최성일 한완상씨 활동주목돼

민통연합에서 앞으로 활동은

문동환회장, 주우정·한완상 부회장, 최성일 사무총장등이 주축이 될것이라는 게 공통된 견해다.

민통연합은 문동환 회장을 중심으로한 동교계 에서의 활동, 주우정, 최성일씨 중심의 미국 민주당 및 학계, 정계 상대의 활동, 한완상씨의 교포사회 및 미국학계 순회 강연 그리고 김대중씨를 보좌하는 역할 을 할것으로 예상된다.

민통연합과 가장 관련이 깊은 독립신문의 김경재에도 능력이 있지만 현재 언론사업 이란 재정적 뒷받침이 뒷받아야 하는것이기 때문에 그의 역할은 예견하기가 쉽지않다.

문동환·최성일·한완상씨는 지난 1년동 안 ① 한민동과 국민회의를 통합시켜 민통 연합을 탄생시키는 산파역할을 맡었고 ② 민 통연합의 재정적 면을 적은규모이긴 조직화 시켜 놓았고 ③ 민통연합내의 의심세력 접근을 봉쇄했고 ④ 대미 활동등이 활발 하여

공로를 인정받고 있다.

새로 부회장에 취임한 주우정 박사는 「에드워드 케네디」 상원의원과 한국인 가운데 가장 친절한 관계를 갖고 있는것으로 알려져 영향력이 적지않으며 학계 정계를 상대로 오래동안 활약해왔고 잠시 한민 신보의 회장을 맡기도 했 었다.

그러나 여기서 꼽히는 4명의 중추적 인사들이 하는 일에는 한계가 있을것이기 때문에 그 이외의 회원들이 이들의 활동을 적극 뒷받침하거나 적극 능력을 발휘 하지

않는한 민통연합이 국내의를 크게 돕을 지 킬만큼 파문을 던질 경우는 기대하기 어려 울것 이라는 견해가 지배적이다.

민통연합이 안으로 안고있는 과제가운데 하나는 역시 「내부명정」 이라고 지적하는 사람도 있다. 이번 정기총회에서 문동환 회 장이 재선되기 까지에는 한승인씨와 표대결 을 하여 4표차이로 이겨야 하는 과정을 밞아나 했다.

김대중씨로 부터도 마찬가지 인것으로 알려졌다. 김씨도 국내라면 몰라도 미국 에서의 수입은 대학강연, 친지들의 회사탕이 전 부라고 한다. 이 수입으로 김씨는 가족들과 비서진을 이끌어야 하고 자신의 활동비활동을 당해야 한다. 김씨에게 민통연합을 도울 여력은 고사하고 오히려 민통연합의 지원을 받아야 할 입장이니 민통의 자금문제 해결은 시원한 길이 보이지 않는게 분명한것 같다.

민통연합이 어떤 활동을 어떻게 전개할것 이며 그 여파가 어디까지 미칠것인지 역시 흥미를 끄는게 사실이다.

민통연합 임원진 명단 (경칭약, 무순)

고   문: 김재준, 김상돈, 한승인
의   장: 문동환
부 의 장: 주우정, 한완상, 김신형
사무총장: 최성일
상임위원: 임정규, 동원모, 김정순, 김동건
         김 경, 김경재, 김용배, 구춘회
         김마태, 곽노순, 이돈만, 이학인
         이재택, 이군원, 이하전, 이상철
         이승만, 임병규, 명주희, 박찬응,
         유시홍, 손명걸, 김팡정, 조옹규
         장지원, 서유웅 및 각 지방 위원
         장.
감   사: 김윤철, 정의순
         김경재

United States Senate
WASHINGTON, D.C. 20510

October 13, 1983

Dr. Woo Jung Ju
Professor of History
Elizabeth City State University
Elizabeth City, North Carolina 27909

Dear Dr. Ju:

I was pleased to hear from you and to have your comments about U.S. Korean relations.

Due to limitations of staff and the demands of responding to my own constituency in Tennessee, I am unable to respond in detail to all of the mail my office receives. I do regret the restraints placed on personal correspondence by the volume of mail and legislative activity. However, I did want to acknowledge your recent letter and assure you that I value the views of all who take the time to share their comments. I continue to rely on the input which my staff and I receive, and I will make every effort to represent your concerns as the Senate considers significant legislation and decisions.

Again, thank you for taking the time to contact me. I appreciate your interest and concern.

Sincerely,

Howard H. Baker, Jr.

HHBJr/lpz

미주동아

1986년 5월27일 화요일

모국 대학교수들의 시국선언지지

김웅수, 주우정박사등 일단의 재미대학교수들 성명발표
한국사회에 만연된 난제들은 비민주적제도에 연유

김웅수, 강석원, 고병철박사등 일단의 재미대학교수들은 21일 「모국 대학 교수들의 시국선언을 전폭적으로지지한다」고 밝히고 「국가존립마저 위태롭게 하는 사회에 만연된 절박한 난제들은 근본적으로 비민주적 사회경제 정치제도에 연유되었다는 그들의 주장에 정국을 주도해야 할 인사들은 겸허한 자세로 귀를 기우리기 바란다」고 촉구했다.

제1차 서명자 39명의 이름으로 된 성명에서 이들 교수진은 「가파른 시국을 수습하는 방안은 국민이 원 하는 민주화의 방향이 전기되어있는 이상 현 정권의 시국에 대한 올바른 인식과 국민의 뜻에 따르는 대결단만이 요망된다」고 강조했다.

성명은 또 「참된 민주화의 적극적 추진만이 국민간에 팽배한 불신감을 없애고 우리의 역사를 정진케 하는 최선의 길」이라고 밝히고 시국선언에 참여한 모국의 대학교수들에게 정신적 지원을 아끼지 않겠다고 다짐했다.

◇ 서명교수는 아래와같다.

강석원 고병철 고 원
길영환 김광정 김영배

김영연 김웅수 김유기
김희진 노광해 동원모
민병휘 박대인 방창모
부성래 유종근 유 혁
윤종건 이동진 이상오
이재원 이재현 이호영
이홍영 임관하 조영환
조웅규 주우정 차만재
최기일 최연홍 최창규
탁운숙 허원무 송석중
심기련 이성형 박성대

(제1차 서명자로 무순)

72

**STATEMENTS BY SENATOR EDWARD M. KENNEDY
FOR HUMAN RIGHTS AND DEMOCRACY IN KOREA**

SENATOR KENNEDY RELEASES LIST OF POLITICAL PRISONERS AND CALLS ON PRESIDENT CARTER TO PRESS FOR HUMAN RIGHTS DURING FORTHCOMING VISIT TO KOREA: JUNE 25, 1979.

Mr. President, following the upcoming summit with major allies in Tokyo, President Carter plans to visit the Republic of Korea from June 29 to July 1. That visit will give the President an opportunity to reaffirm the continuing strong commitment of the United States to the security and well-being of South Korea. But it will also give President Carter a major opportunity to press for substantial improvements in the human rights conditions of the Korean people, whose fate has been closely intertwined with ours since over 54,000 Americans gave up their lives for the freedom of the Korean people in the Korean War.

I have long admired the Korean people for their love of liberty and commitment to social justice. I have also been impressed with South Korea's rapid economic growth, but I have been disturbed by the human cost and unequal distribution of the benefits that have accompanied this growth.

Americans have watched, with deep and growing concern, the progressive deterioration of democracy and human rights in South Korea since President Park Chung Hee imposed the so-called Yushin political system in 1972. The Park government has south to deflect this concern by pointing to far worse conditions which certainly prevail in North Korea under Kim Il Sung. No one questions that North Korea is a personalist totalitarian state in which political and civil rights are much more severely controlled than in the South, and Americans strongly oppose human rights violations in North Korea and in other parts of the world.

We are not, however, supporting North Korea and lending our prestige to President Kim Il Sung. By contrast, we are providing substantial support for South Korea.

In South Korea, the Yushin Constitution places all power in

74

the hands of General Park Chung Hee, president for life. The President is the chairman of the ceremonial body which elects him; he appoints the members of the Central Election Committee which oversees elections; he appoints one third of the National Assembly directly and selects another one-third through his control of the nomination of the government party candidates; he may dissolve the National Assembly at any time; he has the power to appoint, dismiss, and discipline all judges; and he appoints and removes all the members of the constitutional committee which putatively determines whether the laws passed by the National Assembly are constitutional. Should these arrangements be deemed inadequate by the President, he can take emergency measures regarding any of the affairs of the state, whenever, in his judgment, "the national security or the public safety and order is seriously threatened or anticipated to be threatened."

Indeed, President Park has found it necessary to counter an intensifying struggle for human rights and the restoration of democracy through a series of such emergency measures, the capstone of which is Emergency Measure No. 9.

This draconian presidential decree is all-embracing. It prohibits "fabricating of disseminating false rumors." It also bans all criticism of the Yushin Constitution, all unauthorized student activities and even what it calls "defamation" of the decree itself. Furthermore, the government can order any school, organization or business firm to expel or dismiss any student or employee who has violated the decree, and can even close down or suspend any such institution. Violation of the decree or of government orders based on it is punishable by imprisonment for not less than one year. The decree specifically provides that violators can be arrested or searched without a warrant. Those prosecuted for the dissemination of so-called false rumors under this decree are regularly denied the opportunity to call witnesses to prove the truth of their utterances.

Thousands of the Korean people have been subjected since 1972 to arbitrary arrest, torture and long-term incarceration under inhuman conditions for violation of this decree and other statutes which constitute the repressive control apparatus for the Yushin political system. The lack of judicial independence assures conviction in all political prosecutions. The exact number of political prisoners at any given time is impossible to determine but I have a list of over 300 presently imprisoned, prepared by the

North American Coalition for Human Rights in Korea, many adopted as prisoners of conscience by Amnesty International, which I am submitting for the record. Suspected opponents of the regime have been routinely harassed, and some have been brutally beaten and in the past hanged without due process of law. Some have died under mysterious circumstances.

Despite efforts to create the impression that political repression in Korea has lessened, and despite the occasional release of batches of prisoners, recent documentation of human rights conditions from Korea by the World Council of Churches and the International Commission of Jurists indicates an intensification of internal repression. Every nook and cranny of social life is infested by agents of the various and competing political control organizations. The cost of dissent has become higher than ever. Students who express opposition are not only expelled and banned from entering any other schools, but also excluded from jobs and other meaningful participation in the life of the community. Professors are forced to report on their students' political activities. Last year, eleven professors issued a statement which advocated a more humane and democratic educational system. They were arrested, interrogated and summarily dismissed. One of them was sentenced to four years imprisonment. Pluralist civil institutions have been purged of democrats and liberals who are less than enthusiastic about the Yushin system.

In 1975, scores of reporters were dismissed after demanding freedom of the press. They have been harassed and hunted down ever since because they have published occasional newsletters covering important stories excluded from the regular press. On the ninth of May, seven of them were sentenced to terms of up to two and a half years for these activities. People are taken away by unidentified men and their whereabouts remain unknown for weeks. To have and express concern for human rights is a serious crime in Korea. Those who speak out against the human rights violations by the government have been put under surveillance, harrassed, quarantined and often brutally beaten.

Repression in Korea is harshest against ministers, priests, and intellectuals who try to improve the condition of the workers and the poor. The persecution of the Reverend Cho Wah Soon is a case in point. This clergywoman has been hauled in for interrogation no fewer than three hundred times and branded a Communist because of her work with female, teenage sweatshop workers. When these young workers attempted to elect their own union representatives, they were beaten, abused, smeared with human excrement and fired. Pictures of one hundred and twenty-six of them have been circulated throughout the nation lest an unwary employer hire any of them. Reverend Cho tried to help them by taking up their cause and running a handicraft show in her mission. For these activities and her protest against a court's handling of a group of indicted working girls, she is serving a five-year sentence.

Recently seven people who have been active in the labor and agrarian training programs of the respected Christian Academy were arrested, brutally interrogated and indicted for violation of the Anti-Communist Law, another catch-all instrument in the Yushin arsenal. The outcome of their trial is a forgone conclusion. No one prosecuted for a political offense has been acquitted on all courts since the advent of the Yushin political system in 1972.

Political offenders have been tortured to obtain confessions or information, to bring their stories into line with one another, or simply to teach them a lesson. Young women have been grabbed by the hair, and banged against tables and walls. The police have beaten girls on the face until they are completely bruised and swollen. Some have been hit with baseball bats, and indecently handled. One priest was beaten unconscious and dumped into the street. On September 22, 1978 the police viciously attacked a group of Christian leaders, human rights advocates and fired workers who were conducting a peaceful prayer meeting in the Christian Building, headquarters of the Korean National Council of Churches. Political prisoners have been beaten by the prison guards, denied adequate medical treatment and even the infrequent family visit allowed by the rules. They are frequently given rotten food and held in solitary confinement.

In one such incident on April 19 of this year, over 30 students who shouted slogans in support of the 1960 student revolution were severely beaten by prison officials, including the deputy warden, at West Gate Prison. In an apparent attempt to spread fear in the dissident community their parents were allowed to view their two injured children, but when the parents undertook to publicize the story, the police cracked down at once. One should call things by their proper names: the Republic of Korea is a veritable police state. The United States, committed to the defense of its security, stands in constant danger of also supporting the repression of its people.

The Park government justifies this systematic repression by citing the need for unity and strong leadership to promote economic development and to face the menace of a belligerent North Korea. It seems clear, however, that economic development was well underway long before the enactment of the Yushin Constitution. More fundamentally, it is my view that repression promotes disunity between the people and their government. I know that many Korean opponents of the Park government share this view, and many fear that the government's repression is undermining the will of the South Korean people to oppose the totalitarian system of the North.

The only genuine political security comes from the support of the people. Governments cannot last indefinitely without it. The Park government claims the overwhelming support of the Korean people. Yet it has rigged the political system to prevent a free electoral process. The 1978 parliamentary elections are a case in point. Despite circumstances overwhelmingly favorable to government party candidates, the opposition party polled more votes than the government party, but the rigged system did not allow the opposition to assume control of the National Assembly. It is this kind of political manipulation which must inevitably erode popular support of the government.

Koreans are exceptionally warm, intelligent and hard-working people with a proud cultural tradition and a long history of struggle for independence and democracy. Their love of liberty is passionate and deep. Long before we had any presence in Korea that love was enshrined in their own 1919 declaration. We have contributed to their ideals of freedom. Restoration of democracy and the guarantee of human rights seems to be the only alternative to the rise of tension on the volatile peninsula. As long as the schism between government and people which the Yushin system entails continues, the danger of war with the North and the repression exacted in its name will be heightened. Ending this schism will not end the danger of war, but it will reduce the North's temptation to take advantage of this dissent and it would rally the people of the South to wholehearted support of their system and their society.

The political stability of the Republic of Korea can be assured only when its government is based on the voluntary support of the people, not on repression; when the people an freely participate in the political process, not when they are systematically excluded; and when their dignity is respected, not when they are subject to arbitrary arrest, torture and deprivation of livelihood because of their beliefs.

Our experience in Iran and Vietnam have forcibly reminded us of the instability inherent in a government whose repression of its people blocks their voice in their own governmental affairs. United States support will not avail to save such governments. To persist in bolstering a government which 37 American missionaries in Korea recently characterized as "an ailing and oppressive dictatorship" eventually may lead to the same kind of anti-American feeling in Korea which is pervasive today in Iran. The reservoir of good will toward the United States is great in Korea, but it can only be maintained by policies which respond to the needs and aspirations of the Korean people.

The democratic opponents of President Park have uniformly stated that they do not welcome a visit from President Carter under present circumstances, because it will bolster the Korean government's image and encourage the repression which followed President Ford's visit to Korea in 1974. It is therefore essential for President Carter not to appear to embrace the continuing dictatorship and repression of human rights in Korea. There should be no doubt that the United States stands for respect of human rights and restoration of democracy. We may not have the ability to liberate all those who are in chains around the world they have, however, the right to expect us not to appear to endorse their oppressors even if we must continue to do business with those who hold power. Again and again, the consideration of short-term expediencies, benightedness about political sentiments and forces in other countries, and the disproportionate influence of special interests in defining our policies in regard to them have caused serious damage to our relations with the people in those countries.

We must admit that the deep U.S. involvement since World War II has strongly influenced the political forces and leadership of South Korea. The enormity of our military support through the years—More military aid than we have given to any other nation in the our history—had deepened the political repercussions of our presence, unintentionally supporting military interests chary of open and competitive political systems. This involvement through the years gives us a special obligation to be clearly identified with a more liberal and open political process in South Korea. We fail to do so only at our and South Korea's peril.

Unfortunately, the problems between South Korea and the United States did not end with the conclusion of the bribery scandal last year. We must not forget that a major reason for the Park government's efforts to manipulate the Congress and public opinion was to offset its image as a repressive dictatorship. Yet the repression continues, and threatens to undermine the close and strong alliance which we have all supported since the Korean War.

The Carter Administration is committed to the furtherance of human rights and democracy around the world. I strongly support that commitment, and I believe there are few countries in which it can be acted upon more effectively than in Korea.

With the advent of this Administration, the Korean people felt renewed hope in the United States after years of American acquiescence in their government's repression. They welcomed President Carter's statement, during his campaign, that "we cannot look away when a government tortures its people, or jails them for their beliefs," and they welcomed his specific condemnation of human rights in Korea as repugnant to the American people.

We must now keep faith with the Korean people. President Carter's trip can and should be the occasion for major improvements in the human rights situation of that country. Under no circumstances should the Korean people conclude that the purpose or the result of the President's visit was to provide aid and comfort to the Park dictatorship.

For these reasons, I hope that President Carter will take the opportunity of his visit to Korea not only to underline our strong and continuing commitment to the security and well-being of the Korean people—a commitment I strongly support—but also to disassociated the United States from the repressive policies of the Park government and to make clear his deep and persistent concern for human rights and democracy in Korea.

Specifically, I urge President Carter to take the following actions during his visit:

1. Urge President Park to take substantial and irreversible steps to guarantee the basic rights of the Korean people and to restore democracy.

2. State in unmistakable terms, both publicly and privately,

that the strong alliance between our two countries must be founded in shared ideals and values.

3. Meet not only with those in power who seek to use the prestige of his office, but also with those Koreans who struggle for human rights and democracy, and who are being persecuted by the Park government. These people should include at least those who are not currently in jail, such as opposition leaders Kim Young Sam and Kim Dae Jung, Quaker leader Hahm Suk Hon, former president Yun Po Sun, and major religious leaders, especially the Reverend Kim Kwan Suk and Stephen Cardinal Kim.

4. Ask President Park to release all remaining political prisoners, including the famous poet Kim Chi Ha and the over 300 individuals identified in the list I am releasing today.

5. Ask President Park to repeal the infamous, draconian Emergency Measure No. 9 which is the instrument for so much of the continuing repression in Korea.

As the Korean poet Kim Chi Ha said in his "Declaration of Conscience," which was smuggled out of the prison where he is serving a life sentence for his writings:

"Corruption, privilege and dictatorship are a treasure trove for Communism. Preservation of dictatorship and repression does not bring security. Let us face the reality that rejection of dictatorship and oppression brings true security. If we lose freedom and democracy, what is there for us to do then? Shall we risk our lives for a yoke of endless hunger, disease, benightedness and humiliation?"

STATEMENT BY SENATOR KENNEDY
ON REPRESSION IN KOREA:
MAY 22, 1980.

I am deeply concerned by the severe military crackdown in the Republic of Korea, which represents a serious reversal of the initially hopeful trends toward liberalization following President Park's death last October.

Less than five months after lifting the Park regime's hated Emergency Measure Number Nine, South Korea authorities have adopted Martial Law Decree Number Ten. This new, repressive decree extends martial law to the entire country; all political activities and gatherings are proscribed; labor strikes are banned; the universities and the headquarters of both major political parties are closed; criticism of the government is forbidden, and the National Assembly is prevented from convening. Equally disturbing, more than 100 religious, student and, political leaders have been arrested, including opposition leaders Kim Dae Jung and Kim Young Sam and former prime minister Kim Jong Pil.

Two months ago, I expressed my support for continued political liberalization in Korea. But, at the same time, I warned of the danger imposed by the South Korean military under the command of General Chon Too Hwan. Tragically, these warnings proved well-founded, and any hopes for the future of democracy in Korea are now in doubt.

President Choi Kyu Hah has promised that the "political evolution program" which he announced last December "will proceed without change." The South Korean Government should move promptly to end martial law, repeal Martial Law Decree Number Ten, and release all those under arbitrary arrest.

In addition to these urgent steps, I strongly encourage the South Korean Government to complete it's program of political liberalization no later than then end of this year. I would especially welcome the return of government power to civilian control, the lifting of press censorship, the release of all remaining political prisoners, leading to enactments of a democratic constitution, free and open elections, and the formation of a broadly representative cabinet.

The willingness of the South Korean Government to carry out these steps will bear directly upon the future course of our relations. Only by supporting a more liberal and open political system for the Korean people can we help to assure the long-term stability and well-being of the Republic of Korea.

STATEMENT BY SENATOR KENNEDY
ON REPRESSION IN SOUTH KOREA:
JULY 21, 1980.

Following is the text of the statement by Senator Edward M. Kennedy on the continued repression in South Korea. Also attached is a list of the 36 persons to be tried with Kim Dae Jung:

"I am dismayed by the South Korean military's decision to try opposition leader Kim Dae Jung and 36 other persons on charges of violating the anti-sedition, national security, and anti-Communist laws. These charges are clearly fabricated: Mr. Kim's only 'crime' has been to advocate democracy and human rights for the people of South Korea.

"Since his arrest on May 17, Mr. Kim has been denied access to an attorney, and his family and friends have been prevented from seeing him. There are also disturbing reports that Mr. Kim has suffered injuries during interrogation.

"If convicted, the 37 defendants could face the death penalty. This would be an extremely severe setback both to U.S.-South Korean relations and to any hopes for a more democratic society in South Korea. I urge the South Korean Government to reverse its decision and to release Kim Dae Jung and all others under arbitrary arrest.

"It is imperative for the United States to take firm actions to secure the release of Kim Dae Jung and to obtain concrete signs that the South Korean Government will resume its earlier program of liberalization. It would be a sad mistake for this nation to stand idle while the South Korean military goes about establishing a permanent martial-law dictatorship.

"Unless the South Korean authorities are forthcoming in their response, I believe we should be prepared to cancel all official exchanges and visits; recall Ambassador Gleysteen for consultation; and suspend further economic assistance and cooperation with South Korea, including the extension of Ex-Im Bank loans.

"I fully support our continued security commitment to South Korea, but I believe we must make clear to both the South Korean Government and the South Korean people that our support does not extend in any way to political repression and potential destabilization of that country. Only by supporting renewed movement toward a more open and democratic political system for the South Korean people can we assure the long-term stability and security of the Republic of Korea."

This statement follows up Senator Kennedy's May 22 statement which condemned "the severe military crackdown" and called for release of all political prisoners, end of martial law, and return to civilian rule, a democratic constitution, free and open elections and the formation of a broadly representative cabinet.

from the office of

Senator Edward M. Kennedy
of Massachusetts

STATEMENT BY SENATOR KENNEDY
ON REPRESSION IN SOUTH KOREA

FOR MONDAY AM's: July 21, 1980
FOR FURTHER INFORMATION: 202-224-8399
224-2636

Following is the text of the statement by Senator Edward M.
Kennedy on the continued repression in South Korea. Also attached
is a list of the 36 persons to be tried with Kim Dae Jung:

"I am dismayed by the South Korean military's decision to
try opposition leader Kim Dae Jung and 36 other persons on
charges of violating the anti-sedition, national security, and
anti-Communist laws. These charges are clearly fabricated: Mr.
Kim's only 'crime' has been to advocate democracy and human
rights for the people of South Korea.

"Since his arrest on May 17, Mr. Kim has been denied access
to an attorney, and his family and friends have been prevented
from seeing him. There are also disturbing reports that Mr. Kim
has suffered injuries during interrogation.

"If convicted, the 37 defendants could face the death
penalty. This would be an extremely severe setback both to
U.S.-South Korean relations and to any hopes for a more democratic society in South Korea. I urge the South Korean Government to reverse its decision and to release Kim Dae Jung and
all others under arbitrary arrest.

".It is imperative for the United States to take firm actions
to secure the release of Kim Dae Jung and to obtain concrete
signs that the South Korean Government will resume its earlier
program of liberalization. It would be a sad mistake for this
nation to stand idle while the South Korean military goes about
establishing a permanent martial-law dictatorship.

86

"Unless the South Korean authorities are forthcoming in their response, I believe we should be prepared to cancel all official exchanges and visits; recall Ambassador Gleysteen for consultation; and suspend further economic assistance and cooperation with South Korea, including the extension of Ex-Im Bank loans.

"I fully support our continued security commitment to South Korea, but I believe we must make clear to both the South Korean Government and the South Korean people that our support does not extend in any way to political repression and potential destabilization of that country. Only by supporting renewed movement toward a more open and democratic political system for the South Korean people can we assure the long-term stability and security of the Republic of Korea."

This statement follows up Senator Kennedy's May 22 statement which condemned "the severe military crackdown" and called for release of all political prisoners, end of martial law, and return to civilian rule, a democratic constitution, free and open elections and the formation of a broadly representative cabinet. Senator Kennedy emphasized that "the willingness of the South Korean Government to carry out these steps will bear directly upon the future course of our relations."

LIST OF 36 PERSONS TO BE TRIED WITH KIM DAE JUNG

The Martial Law Command report did not specifically name the 36 other defendants; however, the report did mention 36 persons accused either of being part of an institute established "to take over the government in the of the subversion of the incumbent government" or of receiving sums of money to instigate student riots. The 36 names follow:

Rev. Paik Hyung-kyu	Senior Minister, First Presbyterian Church, Seoul.
Prof. Park Nak-chong	Seoul National University.
Rev. Suh Nam-dong	Professor, Hankuk Theological Seminary.
Mr. Song Kon-ho	Journalist, Chairman of Donga-Ilba Reporters Struggle Committee.
Prof. Lee Hyo-jae	Ewha Women's University.
Prof. Tak Hi-jun	Director, Labor Institute, Sunggyun Kwan University.
Prof. Yu In-ho	Professor.
Mr. im Jae-kyoung	Economics Editor, *Hankuk Ilbo*.
Mr. Yang Ho-min	Editorial Staff, *Chosen Ilbo*.
Rev. Moon Ik-whan	Professor, Hankuk Theological Seminary.
Prof. Ahn Byung Mo	Professor, Hankuk Theological Seminary.
Prof. Han Won Sang	Seoul National University; Editor, *Christian Thought;* Chairman, Korean Student Christian Federation.
Prof. Lee Moon Young	Labor Institute, Korea University; Chairman, Korea Christian Faculty Fellowship.

Mr. Ye Chun-ho	Member of the National Assembly, New Democratic Party.
Mr. Han Sung-hon, esq.	Lawyer; General Secretary, Amnesty International, South Korea Chapter.
Mr. Kim Hong-il	Son of Kim Dae Jung.
Mr. Kim Jonq-wan	Aide of Kim Dae Jung.
Mr. No Kyong-gyu	Aide of Kim Dae Jung.
Mr. Chong Dong-nyon	Student, Chonnam University, Kwangju.
Mr. Shim Jae-chul	Student, Seoul National University.
Mr. Song Ki-won	Student, Chungang University, Seoul.
Mr. Yun Yo-yon	Student, Soongchon University
Mr. Park Song-hyck	Student, Sogang University.
Mr. Shim Jae-kwan	Student, Seoul National University.
Mr. Lee Seung-jong	Student, Hankuk Theological Seminary.
Mr. Park Kae-dong	Student, Korea University.
Mr. Shin Kye-yoon	Student, Korea University.
Mr. Park Il-nam	Student, Korea University.
Mr. Bae Ki-sun	Student, Kukmin University.
Mr. Kim Taek-chun	Student, Sogang University.
Mr. Yun Yong-gun	Student, Hankuk University for Foreign Students.
Mr. Choi Man-jin	Student, Myongji University.
Ms. Ahn Sook	Student, Ewha Women's University
Mr. Cho Tae-won	Student, Pusan University
Mr. Kim Bong-woo	Student, Kyunghee University

SENATOR KENNEDY CALLS FOR REVERSAL OF SENTENCES AGAINST KIM DAE JUNG AND OTHER SOUTH KOREAN OPPOSITION LEADERS: SEPTEMBER 17, 1980.

Senator Kennedy made the following statement today regarding the military court sentences against Kim Dae Jung and other opponents of the South Korean military government:

"If carried out, the death sentence of opposition leader Kim Dae Jung and the harsh sentences meted out to other opponents of the military government in South Korea would be a devastating blow to the course of freedom and democracy in that country. The South Korean authorities should have no illusions that they can allow these sentences to stand without serious implications for both their country and its relationship with the United States. I hope that the Carter Administration will make every possible effort to obtain a reversal of these sentences, and I call upon the South Korean authorities to release the defendants and move rapidly toward complete democracy and full respect for human rights."

ANNIVERSARY OF REPRESSION IN KWANGJU, KOREA: STATEMENT BY SENATOR EDWARD M. KENNEDY, CONGRESSIONAL RECORD, MAY 19, 1981

Mr. President, 1 year ago this week, the encouraging movement toward true democracy in Korea was shattered by a military
coup, the arrest of Kim Dae Jung and hundreds of other political
leaders, and the bloody suppression of Student protest by marital
law troops.

In the city of Kwangju and elsewhere in Cholla province,
hundreds were killed and hundreds more injured, arrested or
forced into hiding after a military siege that lasted over a week.
Military occupation of the city inaugurated a reign of fear that
continues even today. Kim Dae Jund, who was nearly elected
President in 1971, was condemned to death before his sentence
was commuted to life imprisonment, on fabricated charges of fo-
menting this rebellion.

Today, the tragedy of Kwangju is an unhealed wound in the
politics of South Korea. It will not be healed until all those who
became political prisoners during this period, especially those
whose "crime" consisted of trying to mediate between civilians
and the military, are released. It will not be healed until freedom
of expression, especially for the press and the media, is guaranteed.

It will not be healed until opposition leaders are permitted
to participate freely in the political process of their nation, and
until the movement toward democracy is resumed with the full
participation and support of the people of South Korea.

There is and can be no doubt that the people of North Korea
have had to endure decades of brutal treatment under a totalitarian dictatorship. For from serving as a pretext for repression
in the South, however, this fact should spur the South Korean
Government to protect and increase its people's freedoms, and to
dramatize the contrast with the North.

91

As true friends and allies of South Korea, we should never ignore the harsh conditions of the North: but we must also recognize the closeness of our relationship with the South and offer our constant encouragement and support to those who pursue freedom in that land.

I remain convinced that the United States must be concerned for human rights in Korea, for without the willing support of a government by its people, both security and freedom itself are in peril.

We maintain our security commitment to the Republic of Korea not only because of our national interest in peace and stability in Asia, but because of our continuing dedication to fundamental values of liberty and justice upon which our Nation was founded. That should be our cause in America, in Korea, and in all parts of the world where men and women yearn to be free.

from the office of

Senator Edward M. Kennedy

of Massachusetts

ADDRESS OF SENATOR EDWARD M. KENNEDY
UNIVERSITY OF HAWAII
October 10, 1981

It is an honor for me to visit the Manoa Campus and to be the guest of the students at the School of Medicine and the School of Public Health.

President Eliot of Harvard once said that the reason a university is such a valuable storehouse of learning is that each student brings a little knowledge in, and no graduate ever takes any knowledge out.

But that is obviously not true here, with your outstanding reputation for excellence in education, and your creative vision of the contemporary role of America toward Asia and the Pacific.

I have come here today to discuss that role. But first, let me speak briefly about two other critical current issues.

A few hours ago, half a world away, they laid to rest the man whose dream of peace began a peaceful revolution in the Middle East.

The words of Shaw that my brothers loved are a fitting measure of this man — "Some men see things as they are and say why. I dream things that never were and say, why not?"

A giant of the earth has now returned to the earth. But we in America know — as the people of Egypt and of Israel know — that the dream of Anwar Sadat shall never die.

It is that same cause of peace which is at issue in our own foreign policy and the future of the Pacific Basin.

We must act with the same boldness and bravery Anwar Sadat brought to the crisis in the Middle East as we deal with the greatest issue of our time or any time in human history — the prevention of nuclear war.

Eight days ago, President Reagan announced a new policy on our strategic nuclear forces. Many of his recommendations deserve support. But I believe that some are dangerously unwarranted and decisively unwise.

The President has properly given high priority to protecting the Command, Control and Communications systems for our nuclear forces. The vulnerability of these systems is more serious than any present danger to our land-based missiles, and we must move immediately to reduce it. It makes no sense to spend billions of dollars on ever more complex nuclear missiles, while neglecting the command and control procedures that are even more essential to the credibility and reliability of our deterrent.

I also agree with the President's decision to move ahead with a strong sea-based strategic missile force, including the Trident II missile.

And I agree as well with the President's decision to develop the Stealth strategic bomber for the 1990's.

But I believe it is a serious mistake to revive the discredited, impractical and wasteful B-1 bomber. The issue here is priorities. B-52's fitted with cruise missiles are all we need until the Stealth bomber comes on line. At a time when we are already short-changing our conventional military forces — even to the point of cutting back on ammunition stockpiles in Western Europe — we should not embark on a thirty-billion dollar spending binge for a B-1 bomber that will not be able to penetrate Soviet air defenses.

Three years ago, the B-1 was cancelled because it will be obsolete the day it leaves the assembly line. Nothing has changed since then. It is still a gold-plated airborne Edsel — and it always will be.

93

2

Finally, on M-X the President and the Secretary of Defense deserve credit for rejecting the absurd race-track basing plan, because it offered no real additional protection for our land-based missiles against Soviet attack. The country has been spared a costly and unnecessary scheme that would have been highly destructive of large regions of the Western States. At a time of deep budget cuts in mass transit for cities, it makes no sense to spend billions of tax dollars on a glorified nuclear shell game that is nothing more than mass transit for missiles.

But the President's alternative on M-X has an equally grave strategic drawback. M-X missiles in fixed, hardened silos will be no less vulnerable to Soviet attack than the current Minuteman missiles in such silos. I support research and development on methods that offer genuine hope of protecting our land-based missile force. But I oppose the Reagan M-X plan. Until the question of vulnerability is answered, we should not spend vast amounts on a new type of land-based missile.

Above all, in this Administration, there is too much talk of nuclear war, and not enough action on nuclear arms control. The Achilles heel of the Reagan defense plan is the absence of any genuine commitment to arms limitation. The peril of our present policy is clear. Without controls on the number of nuclear weapons, there may well be no real way to protect our missiles. Our deterrent will be forever chasing its own tail. In the debate ahead, we need a maximum effort for arms control, not a mindless escalation of the arms race. We must follow the road to peace, not the road to humanity's final war.

Let me turn now to my principal topic here — American foreign policy and the future of the Pacific Basin. Few if any regions of the world can take greater pride in recent progress, or see greater promise for the future.

We have come a remarkable distance in remarkably few years. Only a decade ago, America was still at war in Indochina. China was still in the throes of diplomatic isolation and the Cultural Revolution. And Japan was still absorbing the twin shocks of our surprise economic controls and our surprise initiative on China.

Today, past frictions have been smoothed. Old confrontations have turned into new relationships of cooperation — not just in economics and technology, but even in politics and security. For the first time in this century, China, Japan and the United States enjoy friendly, not hostile, relations with each other. Although Communist and non-Communist military confrontations continue in Korea and elsewhere in the region, the major conflicts now are among the Communist states themselves — between China and the Soviet Union, and between China and Vietnam.

Through ASEAN, the nations of Southeast Asia have moved closer to each other and to Japan, China, and the United States. Better than any other region of the world, the countries of Asia have survived the assaults of OPEC and maintained or enhanced their economic growth and their energy security.

In the shorthand of Atlantic Ocean diplomacy, East-West relations mean U.S.-Soviet confrontation and escalation of the arms race. But in the Pacific Basin, East-West relations have the vastly different connotation of a prospering political partnership and accelerating economic growth. Last year, the United States exported $50 billion and imported $71 billion in trade with this new economic colossus. For the first time in our history, U.S. trade with Asia and the Pacific surpassed our trade with any other region.

But behind the glowing numbers lie statistics of a different sort. A recent book is titled "Japan As Number One," because, the author says, "Japan has dealt more successfully with more of the basic problems of post-industrial society than any other country."

A Japanese worker makes 45 cars a year — 67 at Nissan's most modern factory — compared with 25 for an American. He makes 400 tons of steel a year, compared with 250 for an American — not because Japanese workers are more efficient, but because of better plants, better equipment, better techniques of planning and production, and better partnership between government, management, and labor.

I reject the view that American ingenuity has run out, or that we are nearing the end of the American Century, in which our economy can be at the forefront of world progress.

-3-

That is why, long before the Reagan Administration, I called for comprehensive incentives for innovation, investment, and productivity to achieve the reindustrialization of America. I believe that in the 1980's, there is no reason the American economy cannot do as well as, or better than, any other economy on earth.

To some extent, American business must share a portion of the blame for our present unsatisfactory position in the world economy. Often, U.S. firms have been slow to respond to obvious possibilities overseas. Golden opportunities have been lost, as new Asian markets flow to European and other foreign competitors.

But in other cases, American enterprises are shut out by unfair barriers erected by other economies to protect their domestic industries. This year, Japan's trade surplus with the United States will be $15 billion — an unprecedented deficit that impairs the ties between our nations.

Free trade must be a two-way street. Developing countries deserve assistance, and their industries deserve a fair opportunity to reach maturity. But the fairness doctrine also means that American business deserves a fair chance to compete with the Asian economic giants. Parity is a necessity — and in the present troubled state of our economy, I assure you that Congress will demand it.

And I shall do all I can in Congress to ensure that the magnificent environmental heritage we share with all people of the Pacific is not sacrificed on the altar of blind economic growth. In particular, I am proud to stand with you against the incredibly short-sighted schemes of those who would transform these beautiful waters into a blighted basin for the storage of nuclear waste.

Here in these islands, you know the endless promise of energy from the sun and the sea. Already, the "mini-OTEC" experiment at the East-West Center is proving the incredible potential of thermal power from the ocean. Before us lies the possibility of energy security for all time for all nations of the Pacific Basin. Nuclear power is an idea whose time has come and gone. The nuclear way is not the Pacific way.

We must also give greater priority on the Pacific agenda to fundamental issues of security, human rights and human needs.

Asia faces the spectre of growing Soviet military power by sea, air, and land. Despite world-wide condemnation, the Soviet Union continues to occupy Afghanistan. And conflict and turmoil still tear at Cambodia and Laos.

We must do more to meet this security challenge. We must strengthen the military capabilities of our allies in Asia through bilateral treaties and multilateral agreements.

We must press harder for a political settlement, under which the Vietnamese withdraw from Cambodia and the Soviets withdraw from Afghanistan.

Consistent with its post-war constitution and political tradition, Japan must bear a greater part of the burden of its own defense. It can share the costs of our military forces on its territory. It can contribute its innovative technological genius to our pressing security needs. And it can offer greater private and public assistance to speed the development of the poorer Asia nations.

On China, I approve the sale of limited defensive military equipment, such as radar and anti-tank and anti-aircraft weapons, to the Peoples Republic. But we must avoid a military alliance and supply relationship with Peking that could threaten our friends and increase the risks of war between China and the Soviet Union. It was an unnecessary blunder for the Reagan Administration to announce the arms sales without consulting Japan or our other allies.

And, as we improve relations with Peking, we must continue to support the security and well-being of the people on Taiwan.

The search for peace and security in Asia must also be pursued in the arena of human rights.

It was wrong for President Reagan to invite General Chun, the President of South Korea, to Washington and then neglect any mention of the destruction of democracy and the denial of human rights in Korea in the military coup and the subsequent military repression. Over thirty thousand American soldiers gave their lives in the 1950's for the freedom and independence of the people of South Korea. By standing up for human rights in South Korea in the 1980's, we can help ensure that they did not die in vain.

95

-4-

It was also wrong for the Vice President to travel to Manila and pay tribute to
President Marcos for his "dedication to democratic principles and process." And it
will be an even greater wrong for President Reagan to welcome President Marcos to the
White House, without pressing our concern for human rights. The Administration knows
full well the shameful scope of violations of human rights in the Philippines where
elections are meaningless, and where hundreds of innocent men, women and children have
been assassinated by the security forces and their murderous confederates.

To those who say that Asians do not believe in democracy or care about human
rights, I reply: Tell that to the starving victims in the cruel new economic zones
of Vietnam.

Tell it to the inmates of prison camps in China.

Tell it to Wei Jingsheng, imprisoned for 15 years in China. Tell it to Shih
Ming-teh and Reverend C. M. Kao, imprisoned on Taiwan; or the family of Professor
Chen, who died after being released from interrogation there.
Tell it to Kim Dae Jung, imprisoned for life in South Korea, or to the thousands
like him held in North Korea.

They are the silent heroes of human rights, the courageous keepers of the
conscience of our time. Together with their thousands of friends and supporters,
they have kept the flame of hope alive. They are the true patriots of our century
who have pledged their lives, their fortunes, and their sacred honor to the cause
of human independence.

They deserve more from the government of the United States than a quiet diplomacy
of silence and indifference. When human rights are endangered in Asia or any other
region of the world, America must never look the other way.

Nor can we turn our backs on the hundreds of millions of our brothers and sisters
in Asia who lack adequate food, shelter and health care. It is a sad irony that
bellies are most distended, disease is most deadly, and poverty is most pervasive in
Indonesia, the Philippines, and Thailand, whose material resources should rank them
among the richest nations of the world. Nations poorer in natural resources, like
Japan, Singapore and Taiwan, have achieved much higher growth and much fairer distribution of their wealth.

The lesson is clear. More indispensable than any bounty that nature can
provide are human and technological resources. That means decent health care
and housing and education and the other things that make all the difference
in the age-old struggle against ignorance and pestilence and poverty. Above
all else, perhaps, it means integrity in leadership and unyielding resistance
to corruption.

America can do more to seed and nourish these critical human qualities and
resources. We need broader partnerships in many different areas between governments and
universities and private enterprises. Within the nations of this region, we must
make a greater effort to bring public and private interests together and to encourage
more effective means of Pacific cooperation. America has profound political, social,
economic and security interests in the Pacific Basin. What we seek is neither a
grand military alliance nor an all-embracing economic bloc, but a partnership for
peace and progress reflecting the realities of the region and the aspirations of its
peoples.

Leaders of vision in Hawaii are pointing the way to a future of peace and progress
in the Pacific for America and for all nations. Over the generations — from Truman
and MacArthur to Johnson and Westmoreland — American national leaders have come to
Honolulu to plot the course of war in the Pacific.

I look forward to the day when our leaders will come here, to these beautiful
islands, to plan the course of peace in an ocean which bears the name of peace.

I look forward to the time when the Mainland will catch up with Hawaii — and all
Americans will understand that the Pacific is truly the Ocean of the Future.

96

Senate

THE SITUATION IN KOREA

Mr. KENNEDY. Mr. President, in these days of heightened tension in Central America; days of apprehension for the situation in the Middle East; days of quarrels and misunderstandings over the issue of arms control, we cannot forget those areas of the world which have long been of primary importance for American foreign policy. Today, I am thinking specifically of a region to which the United States committed itself in the years 1950-53: the Korean peninsula.

In those years, we fought alongside citizens of many other countries to defend Korea and "make the world safe for democracy." I ask you Mr. President, where is that democracy today?

U.S. rhetoric has not been matched with deeds. The Koreans welcome our friendship and our support. But we must lend that support responsibly; we must insure that our support helps strengthen the ties between the people and their government, and not support repressive policies which only serve to alienate the people and erect barriers between society and official leadership.

Mr. Kim Dae Jung, founder of the Korean Institute for Human Rights and respected leader of the South Korean opposition who came to the United States last year, recently shared with me his optimistic analysis of the present situation in South Korea. According to Mr. Kim:

For peace, in Korea, the most important thing is: establishing a sound government which enjoys the voluntary support of the people. Support from the people will prevent any subversive force from gaining hold in the South and will prevent any possibility of the North's communizing the South. Furthermore, from a position of strength, the South can lead North Korea to dialog and peaceful resolution of problems. The future for peace on the Korean peninsula will be decided on the question of whether the people in the South can restore democratic government and on whether the United States supports such efforts and terminates its present policy of support for military dictatorship.

Mr. President, I ask that the full text of Mr. Kim's most recent addresses on the Korean situation be printed in the RECORD.

The addresses follow:

THE KOREAN PENINSULA—PEACE AND REUNIFICATION

(By Kim Dae Jung)

It is a privilege for me to speak before you at this church—a church which is so closely identified with one of the themes in my talk—that of peace. This church must take pride in the role it has had and in its minister, Rev. Coffin, who has been a leader in the peace movement for a long, long time. He is widely recognized as having been an outstanding figure in the Vietnam peace movement. I believe we may safely call him a prophet of our time as he continues to press for a resolution of the conflict in Central America.

I am touched by and deeply grateful for the role Rev. Coffin and this church took in my personal plight in 1980. I know that on very short notice Rev. Coffin opened this church to a gathering of some 600 people who expressed concern and anger when news of my arrest in May of that year reached here at the time of the Kwangju incident.

It is my hope that Rev. Coffin and this church will continue to play a significant role in the resolution of problems facing my country, Korea.

I. THE CONDITIONS OF PEACE

Technically speaking, the Korean peninsula has continued on in a state of war ever since the truce of July, 1953 because there has been no progress toward a peace treaty. Intense hostility has remained. The number of soldiers and the amount of weaponry has actually increased. The possibility of another conflict has been evident for over thirty years. The United States has maintained tens of thousands of troops in South Korea throughout this period in order to prevent another conflict. However, there has been peace on the peninsula—though it has been tenuous.

I see two major reasons that this peace has been maintained in spite of the poor conditions. First, there has been a balance of power factor not only between the South and the North but also with their respective supporters, the United States and Japan on one side and China and the Soviet Union on the other. As in Europe, the balance of power on the Korean peninsula has helped to keep the peace. The situation in Korea is thus not like that in the Middle East where there is no effective balance of power.

Second, neither side has felt that it could gain any advantage by provoking war and thus upset this balance of power. Each side has felt it would only sustain serious damage should war break out. The damage would destroy the works of great labor which went into building up out of the ashes of war. War has been avoided because there has existed a balance of power and there has been no temptation to gain advantage on either side. These conditions will last long into the future. Thus, I don't see much possibility of another conflict. In addition, China has recently expressed a strong desire to promote peaceful conditions on the peninsula in cooperation with the United States and Japan. The Soviet Union is also unwilling to see any conflict on the Korean peninsula because it can see no advantage in such a conflict.

Last month, North Korea proposed a three-way dialogue revealing a drastic change in attitude. It had strongly opposed any dialogue with South Korea before then and had persistently insisted on having negotiations only with the United States to bring about a peace treaty. There is a great possibility that dialogue involving both South and North Korea will take place this year in spite of present delays. President Reagan's visit to China this April may bring about significant progress toward the start of dialogue. Though I am not sure that a permanent peace treaty can be achieved, I believe that dialogue can ease the tensions and hostility on the peninsula. I know that South Korea on the one hand and China and the Soviet Union on the other have hopes of establishing trade ties. It is known that North Korea also has a desire to develop economic relations with western countries. There is talk that North Korea is preparing a free port for this purpose on its west coast. Such economic relations could greatly help to maintain peace on the Korean peninsula.

However, there is a serious factor which if uncorrected can certainly damage the balance of power on the peninsula and the national security of South Korea. Since South Korea is under dictatorial rule, there is no guarantee of freedom of speech, academic freedom, freedom to organize and participate in trade unions, and elections of true value. There is a rubber stamp opposition party, National Assembly, and judicial branch. The more the economy grows, the greater is the gap between the haves and the have-nots, between urban and rural areas, between big enterprises and small enterprises, and between regions. Ten tycoon businessmen alone control 50% of the GNP. Therefore, the people's dissatisfaction has seriously increased. Consequently the present military regime can not enjoy the people's support and the United States is being criticized as the main support of this evil government. North Korea is eager to take advantage of the situation, but I don't see much chance that North Korea will stage an invasion across the DMZ. As Congressman Stephen Solarz has said North Korea will become ever bolder in seeking to promote turmoil by agitating dissatisfied people. Without improvement toward democracy there is no doubt that turmoil will become common and continue. Thus, North Korea may have a chance to create another Vietnam-like situation.

The clearest danger to peace is within South Korea. For peace, the most important thing is not good negotiations with the North but establishing a sound government which enjoys the voluntary support of the people. Only democratic government can gain the people's full support and ask for the people's dedication in maintaining stability and security. This is so because democratic government can guarantee the freedom, justice, and human dignity to which the Korean people have so long aspired. Support from the people will prevent any subversive force from gaining hold in the South and will prevent any possibility of the North's communizing the South. Furthermore, from a position of strength, the South can lead North Korea to dialogue and peaceful resolution of problems. The future for peace on the Korean peninsula will be decided on the question of whether the people in the South can restore democratic government and on whether the United States supports such efforts and terminates its present policy of support for military dictatorship.

Another important factor is on an international level. Support for peace must come from the four big powers, the United States, the Soviet Union, Japan and China, which have geographical and traditional interests in the region. So, a three-way dialogue alone will not be sufficient. It must develop toward a six-way dialogue.

In a word, restoration of democracy and four-power cooperation are essential for peace on the Korean peninsula.

II. PROSPECTS FOR REUNIFICATION

Unlike the two Germanys, both Koreas have taken unification as their main goal. Unification has been persistently supported internationally. The four powers, the United States, the Soviet Union, Japan and China, which have strong interests in and influence on the peninsula now also support unification officially. In spite of the lack of opposition to unification, we have failed to achieve it in forty years time and there is no strong hope that we may achieve this goal in the near future.

There are two reasons for failure to achieve unification. First, even though the four powers support unification, they have not been truly interested in the realization of unification due to the nature of the cold war. They have not wanted to see any change in the balance of power in the peninsula and unification might upset it. The strategic importance of the peninsula is perceived as critical. The four powers have preferred to maintain the status quo with the peninsula divided in two. There is no real possibility of establishing a unified and neutral government such as that in Austria. Second, the persistent ambition of North Korea to communize South Korea and South Korea's continuing fear of North Korea have prevented moves toward peaceful unification. There has been no mutual trust, no progress toward reduction of hostilities between the two sides, no progress toward the restoration of a national consensus. There is a significant difference in the two systems' political, economic, and social development over the last forty years, and so we can see little possibility of early peaceful reunification as one country under the present circumstances.

3

To achieve peaceful unification we must succeed in addressing two areas of concern— a local one and an international one.

First, in South Korea, we must establish a strong and truly stable government with the people's cooperation and full support via the implementation of democracy. Such a government may have meaningful dialogue with North Korea in working toward the realization of peaceful coexistence and move toward a loose federal system as a first step. The existence of the communist government in the North could be recognized on one hand while South Korea would have to be guaranteed its right to exist as a democratic government on the other. The greater the increase of mutual trust and negotiation, the farther along we may proceed toward establishing one country under a loose federal systems.

Second, on an international level, though we think of unification as something to be solved by the 60 million Koreans in the South and North, we can not deny that there is a strong influence coming from the four powers affecting the goal of unification. Each of the big powers has serious misgivings about a unified Korea. Each fears that a unified Korea might damage its security or other interests. The four powers may maneuver to thwart our efforts for the realization of unification thus augmenting the anti-unification factors within the South and the North. Whether we like it or not, we can not, therefore, ignore international attitudes though we should maintain a strong national determination to work toward one Korea.

Fundamentally speaking, peace and unification should be gained with the aid of the Korean people's strength. When there is a government in the South which is strong, North Korea will be cooperative in working toward the realization of peace and unification. When there is such a strong government in the South, the four powers will not be able to disregard the Korean people's desire for peace and reunification. Such strength must come from democratic government which can enjoy the people's full support. But, unfortunately, there is now no such democratic government in the South. This is mainly because of United States support for the present military dictatorship. It is well-known that while enjoying little support from the Korean people, General Chun can maintain his power only with United States support. United States support has led to Japanese support. Such international support for dictatorship has seriously discouraged democratic elements in the military and among our people. Though the United States has justified its support of military dictatorship using maintenance of peace as an excuse, this stand has backfired and peace is now actually threatened because dictatorship has greatly destroyed our people's loyalty. There is also a growing anti-American feeling among our people because of United States failure to support the cause of democracy in the South. If the present situation continues, we can not avoid meeting a fate similar to that seen in Vietnam: The present feeble peace may not be maintained and South Korea may be communized by the North.

I am not asking the United States to restore democracy in our stead; we only ask the United States not support military dictatorship but lend moral support to our democratic cause. With such moral support, we can achieve democratic government and work toward peace and eventually toward reunification.

As I said at the beginning of this talk, this church under the guidance of Rev. Coffin is a world-renowned force for peace. You base your belief and work for peace in God's love. I sincerely ask you to impress your government and the American people to support the Korean people's efforts. We can succeed with your help.

I thank you.

THE PRESENT SITUATION IN KOREA
(By Kim, Dae Jung)

You are all knowledgeable in Asian affairs and particularly well-versed in Korean issues. As a Korean who has long been imprisoned and thus separated from Korean society and now one who has been away from Korea for more than one year, I should be the one receiving information from you on the present Korean situation. In Korean, we say this is like preaching Buddhism to Buddha. Recognizing my shortcomings in this regard, I will tell you briefly what I know of the present situation in South Korea to set the stage for the question and answer period which is to follow.

I want to address five areas. They are: 1) the issue of talks between North and South Korea as proposed by North Korea; 2) the necessity of systematic reform for human rights; 3) the possibility of another Yushin System; 4) the possibility of conflict between students and the government; and 5) the present role of the Korean churches.

I. THE ISSUE OF TALKS BETWEEN NORTH AND SOUTH KOREA

Last month North Korea made an unexpected proposal for three-way dialogue involving both Koreas and the United States. A similar proposal for a three-way dialogue was put forward by the late Park Chung Hee and President Carter in 1979 when President Carter visited Seoul. In spite of this, the attitudes of South Korea and the United States toward the present North Korean proposal are not very positive. The United States prefers to have a four-way dialogue which would include China. South Korea insists on a bilateral dialogue between the South and the North while leaving open the possibility of a four-way or six-way dialogue which would include the Soviet Union and Japan. South Korea is firmly resisting participation in a three-way dialogue even at the risk of contradicting its stand of 1979 when a proposal for such talks was issued from South Korea. South Korea worries about being excluded if North Korea should concentrate its efforts on dealing with the United States alone. North Korea might justify such an attitude on the grounds that it was North Korea and the United States which signed a truce agreement to end the Korean War in 1953.

On the other hand, North Korea is strongly opposed to a four-way dialogue. Two reasons can be cited. One is to avoid the dissatisfaction of the Soviet Union by participating in talks which would only involve China and not the Soviets. The other reason is to prevent South Korea's long-held desire of establishing contacts with China. The

4.

North Koreans are not likely to support a six-way dialogue at present either. The North Korean proposal for a three-way dialogue is supported by the Soviet Union.

The coming visit of President Reagan to China may result in decisive progress on this issue.

I see a strong possibility of opening some type of dialogue this year. However, I think that if there is a firm guarantee of equal status for South Korea at a three-way conference, that the three-way dialogue would be most likely.

My position is not in opposition to any type of dialogue as a first step to easing tensions on the Korean peninsula, but I firmly believe that only a six-way dialogue can produce any progress toward peace on the Korean peninsula because all four powers, the United States, Japan, China, and the Soviet Union, have vital interests and strong influence in Korea. Without their combined cooperation, we can never expect real peace on the Korean peninsula. This has been my persistent position since the 1971 Korean presidential election when I proposed four-power cooperation on the Korean peninsula.

II. THE NECESSITY OF SYSTEMATIC REFORM FOR HUMAN RIGHTS

The State Department has pointed out improvement in the Korean human rights situation in 1983 as compared with previous years. This came in its annual report on human rights. It mentioned the release of political prisoners—mainly students—and the granting of permission for students to return to their respective campuses. Of course, I also welcomed these moves, but this does not constitute a fundamental improvement in the human rights situation because many times in Korea we have seen the repeated release and imprisonment and the repeated expulsion and re-entry of students to college campuses. Without systematic reform toward a guarantee of human rights, we can never say that there is improvement in human rights. What we see is rather the cosmetic tactics of dictatorial rule in cheating public opinion both domestically and internationally. We need legal guarantees for the democratic rights of assembly, academic freedom, freedom for labor to organize, and freedom for farmers to form cooperatives. Of all freedoms, the freedom of speech and the freedom to have fair elections are the most essential core elements in guaranteeing human rights. When there is freedom of speech, any violation of human rights can be publicly criticized. When there is a fair system of elections, any government which can not guarantee human rights or which violates human rights will be voted out of office. The South Korean regime of Chun Doo Hwan strongly opposes any systematic reform—especially anything moving toward freedom of speech and free elections. The regime strongly opposes abolition of the notorious basic law governing the mass media, and government dominated elections laws. Further, it refuses to lift the ban imposed on 300 political figures. This ban prohibits these figures from making any public speeches or participating in any election activities.

III. THE POSSIBILITY OF ANOTHER YUSHIN SYSTEM

As you may remember, Park Chung Hee abused the South/North dialogue coming out of the July 4, 1972 joint communique. He proclaimed the Yushin System—justifying it as necessary to promote reunification, but from the time of the proclamation of the Yushin System until his death in 1979—a period of seven years—the Yushin System only served to shore up his dictatorial regime.

In spite of General Chun's repeated pledges to step down from office in March of 1988 after serving one term, there is a strong possibility that he seeks to continue his rule after 1988. There is a possibility of political maneuvering this year. Something which indicates that this is so is a move by the rubber stamp opposition parties for direct election of the president. The rubber stamp mass media has given full coverage to this idea. In South Korea without government approval, no opposition party or press organization can put forward such an idea. Chun was elected indirectly. A direct election after a constitutional amendment could be justified by Chun as a necessity in facing North Korea in talks. That is, Chun could say he needed to prove his popular support in order to face the North. Such a direct election under present conditions without freedom of speech and fair elections could easily be orchestrated by the government.

I predicted that Park Chung Hee would abuse the unification issue as a means to have himself elected for life. I made this prediction in 1970 and 1972. In 1972, the Yushin System was put in place and confirmed my prediction. I now see a similar possibility under the Chun regime.

IV. THE POSSIBILITY OF CONFLICT BETWEEN STUDENTS AND THE GOVERNMENT

Student power has grown tremendously through years of bitter experience and ordeal. Students are firmly determined to fight against dictatorship. Most of our people are different than they were in 1980. They now support the students' cause.

Expelled studnets are being forced to sign pledges of repentance before they may return to the campuses. However, the majority of these students refuse to do this, saying that they have nothing to repent for and that what they have stood for is an open advocacy of democracy which is not wrong. At the same time, there are signs that the government seeks to stir up trouble among students so that it may have an excuse to strongly repress them this coming spring. The government has been letting statements out from unidentified sources which accuse students of being leftist or pro-communist. The government has always used the charge of communism to crack down on its rivals. You know that in Korea this is a very serious charge which may easily turn some people against the students. I believe we must exercise caution at this critical time to avoid playing into the government's hands. We should be on our guard against such plots by the government and not be abused by such things.

100

V. THE PRESENT ROLE OF THE KOREAN CHURCHES

Korean churches have played a central role in the restoration of democracy and human rights movement since Park Chung Hee proclaimed the Yushin System in October, 1972. The role of churches has been significant and decisive in maintaining our movement. Recently, there have been signs of a lessening of the churches' role and there has been criticism—especially among students—of the role played by the churches because of the churches' pro-American attitude and the reluctance of the churches to continue their courageous role as they, as individuals, did before with prayer meetings and in rising imprisonment because of their stands. I don't think these criticisms are necessarily correct, but there is some indication of weakness in the church movement for democracy and human rights. On the other hand, some young men are showing signs of impatience. Patience is very necessary in enduring such periods of trial and in dealing with the short-tempered military regime.

Even though there are some arguments between church and non-church groups, we still have the same strong goal of realizing democracy. All recognize this as most important. Democracy is necessary in order to realize national security without the presence of American troops and to have a dialogue with North Korea with full confidence that a peaceful solution may be realized. To promote mutual understanding, joint activities involving church and non-church groups are essential in order to achieve our goal and not give any room for abuse by the shrewd maneuvering of the government.

I came here in December of 1982. During this last year I have devoted myself totally to persuading the United States government and friends not to support the military dictatorship in Korea. I believe it is harmful to the United States to support the dictatorship. For stability and security in Korea and for friendly relations between the people of Korea and the United States such support is also harmful. In spite of the Chun Doo Hwan government's lack of support from the people as reported in the American press, the Chun regime is maintained mainly because of United States support. As the United States supports the regime so does Japan. Because the United States and Japan support the Chun regime, democratic elements in the military and among our people have been greatly discouraged. Now, the United States has become a target of criticism and even hatred among our people. I really worry about this phenomenon for both Korea and the United States. My main purpose in being here in the United States is to persuade the United States to change its policy. I seek American public support.

We must avoid another debacle such as seen in Vietnam. As I first mentioned, you are well informed about the Korean situation and I believe you will share my worries about the present situation. Let's focus our attention and energies to impress your government to change its policies.

STATEMENT BY SENATOR EDWARD M. KENNEDY ON THE FIGHT FOR HUMAN RIGHTS IN KOREA MAY 17, 1984

This week we commemorate the fourth anniversary of the Korean military authorities' bloody suppression of citizen protest in Kwangju. It was four years ago this week that students and other Korean citizens took to the streets in Kwangju and elsewhere in Cholla province to protest a military coup and the imposition of martial law in Korea. A week-long military siege of the city left hundreds killed, and many hundreds more injured, arrested or forced into hiding.

Over one hundred graves in an unmarked corner of the main public cemetery east of Kwangju remain as a solemn reminder of that repression. Bitterness continues to run deep. "There is a lot of pain and hurt that has not healed," Kwangju's Roman Catholic Archbishop observed recently. Earlier this month, Pope John Paul II paid an important visit to Kwangju. The Pope spoke of "the deep wounds that pain your hearts and souls from personal experiences and from recent tragedies, which are difficult to overcome from merely a human point of view, especially for those of you from Kwangju."

There have been some welcome developments in Korea over the past year. The Korean government released several hundred political prisoners—mainly students. The civil rights of several hundred former political prisoners were restored. And the government released over two hundred politicians from the 8-year ban on participation in political activities which it imposed in 1980. The South Korean government also modified its tactics for countering student portest. The government, according to press reports, offered to let students expelled for anti-government demonstrations return to classes, removed official police from campuses and turned campus discipline over to university authorities.

But these moves do not constitute fundamental improvement

in the human rights situation. Let us not forget the several hundred political prisoners who remain in jail under difficult conditions. Let us not forget the 99 persons who are still banned from political activity—including such prominent political leaders as Kim Dae Jung, Kim Young Sam and Kim Jong Pil. Let us not forget reports that the Korean government has pressed some of the more outspoken student critics into military service, six of whom reportedly died during military duty. And let us not forget that freedom of expression remains suppressed.

Nor can we forget the much more severe conditions of repression that prevail in North Korea. Not only are human rights and democracy an anathema to the totalitarian regime of Kim Il Sung, but that regime persists in its terrorist policies against South Korea—including last October's appalling assassination of numerous South Korean government leaders in Rangoon, an action that confirms the North's standing as an international outlaw.

The United States remains strongly committed to the security of the Republic of Korea. But that security commitment must never be the pawn of political ambition. Nevertheless, we can and we must continue to press for progress in democracy and freedom in South Korea—for which over 30,000 Americans lost their lives during the Korean War.

Steps taken over the past year fall short of the true goal we all must have in South Korea: the climate of repression must end, and respect for human rights and democracy must be strenthened. South Korean authorities should carry out their professed intention to lift restrictions on a broad range of freedoms, including political activity by opposition leaders. This is the path toward healing the pain in Kwangju.

Mr. Kim Young Sam, the former leader of the now outlawed New Democratic Party, staged a hunger strike last year "to show we must expand out fight for democracy." And Mr. Kim Dae Jung, South Korea's most prominent political exile, stated in a recent speech in New York: "We need legal guarantees for the democratic rights of assembly, academic freedom, freedom for labor to organize, and freedom for farmers to form cooperatives. Of all freedoms, the freedom of speech and the freedom to have fair elections are the most essential core elements in guaranteeing human rights."

Pope John Paul II began his visit to Korea earlier this month by expressing the hope that South Korea's economic progress would lead to "a more humane society of true justice and peace." The Pope set as a goal to which South Korea should aspire a country "where to govern is to serve, where no one is used as a tool, no one left out and no one downtrodden, where all can live in real brotherhodd."

On this anniversary of the Kwangju uprising, let us reflect upon the Pope's message. And let us express our hopes that these goals will be realized in Korea without further delay.

STATEMENT BY SENATOR EDWARD M. KENNEDY INTRODUCING THE DEMOCRACY IN SOUTH KOREA ACT OF 1987 JUNE 18, 1987

Today, we are beginning a new and stronger phase of our efforts in Congress to support human rights and democracy in South Korea. The legislation we are introducing calls for a suspension of three current economic subsidies to that country.

The United States has important security interests in South Korea. Thirty thousand Americans died in the 1950's to defend those interests, and we do not intend their sacrifice to be in vain. South Korea continues to face a serious threat from North Korea. Forty thousand American troops are stationed in the South to guarantee its defense and to emphasize that our commitment to the security of that nation remains solid and unwavering. But South Korean today is threatened not only from without, but from within.

For over three decades the people of South Korea have struggled to achieve a prosperous, stable and democratic country. In fact, Korea has already accomplished one of the great post-war economic miracles. Yet the government in Seoul continues to maintain that its citizens are not ready for democracy. Patience in South Korea is clearly wearing thin. Now is the time for transition from dictatorship to democracy; unless the government of Korea implements reforms, increased instability, violence and even bloodshed are likely, and the Olympic Games will be in jeopardy—tear gas is not conducive to Olympic competition.

President Chun's unacceptable attempt to dictate the transfer of power on his own terms in 1988 has triggered the current round of massive protest and civil unrest. And for good reason. In an arrogant and authoritarian action last April, he suspended debate on constitutional reform; his recent attempt to install his crony Roh Tae Woo as his successor has again demonstrated his contempt for democracy. The people of Korea understand the stakes—for those actions could well mean the denial of democracy in Korea for seven more years. Students, businessmen, teachers, nuns, and priests have taken to the streets in numbers not seen since the brutal military coup in 1979 and President Chun's rigged election in 1981.

The current situation is both a challenge and an opportunity for the United States and for American diplomacy. Yet the Secretary of State, instead of forthrightly calling for steps toward democracy, urges restraint and tilts toward the regime. Again and again and again, in South Africa, in Chile, and now in Korea, the Reagan Administration has shown its own contempt for the struggle for democracy in other lands. We have learned to our regret in Congress that quiet diplomacy in this Administration means no diplomacy.

Now, in a disgraceful abdication of responsibility, high officials in the State Department plead the pressure of Irangate, the Persian Gulf, and other business, and say they do not have time to deal with South Korea. Well, Congress is busy with these issues too, but we also have time for Korea. Our legislation, the "Democracy in South Korea Act," is designed to fill the vacuum created by the Administration's default, and to place America squarely on the side of human rights and democracy in South Korea. It contains three provisions, which are based on the proposition that in the current situation, there is no justification for American trade assistance that subsidizes dictatorship in South Korea.

First, the bill requires the United States to cast a "no" vote on multilateral development bank loans to south Korea. Current law already requires us to oppose loans to governments that violate basic human rights. President Chun's regime is guilty of physical and psychological torture, arbitrary arrest and detention, house arrest, violation of free assembly and association, and violation of freedom of the press. The respected opposition leader Kim Dae Jung is now under house arrest on the basis of human rights violations; in 1986, we actually voted for $812 million in loans to South Korea.

Second, the bill eliminates existing trade preferences for Korean exports to the United States. The government of South Korea consistently violates international standards on the rights of workers, including the right of association and the right to organize and bargain collectively. Yet the Reagan Administration has determined that Korean exports remain eligible for duty-free and preferential trade treatment under the Generalizes System of Preferences. Current law requires that GSP beneficiaries must at least be taking steps to comply with internationally-recognized workers' rights. In 1986, the U.S. imported $2.2 billion worth of Korean goods under GSP, and this preferential treatment should end.

Third, the bill denies loans, credits, and other guarantees by the Overseas Private Investment Corporation for U.S. investment in Korea. Like GSP, the OPIC law requires recipients to comply with internationally recognized labor standards. Current OPIC guarantees for South Korea total $270 million—second in the world only to Chile.

These provisions will take effect thirty days after enactment of the legislation. The subsidies and loans can be restored after a Presidential certification is approved by Congress, stating that South Korea has made significant progress in meeting international standards of human rights and labor rights and has taken specific steps to bring democracy to Korea.

In intend to give this measure high priority, and to seek its inclusion in the trade bill that the Senate will soon take up.

Obviously, there are differences between South Korea and the Philippines. But there is also a shining similarity—the groundswell of popular support for democracy. Perhaps, in Korea, the dictator can stand against that tide yet again—but there is no excuse for the United States of America to stand beside him. I urge Congress to support this legislation, and I call on the Administration to join us in seeking genuine democracy in South Korea.

STATEMENT BY SENATOR EDWARD M. KENNEDY ON THE AGREEMENT OF THE KOREAN GOVERNMENT TO HOLD DIRECT PRESIDENTIAL ELECTIONS JUNE 30, 1987

A peaceful revolution is taking place in Korea. Over the past three weeks, we have watched a series of dramatic developments in that nation. Day after day, tens of thousands of people poured into the streets, demanding democracy. With the fall of the dictator in the Philippines fresh in mind, the spirit of democracy was ignited in Korea, kindling the flame of freedom in the hearts of workers, nuns and priests, businessmen and women, teachers and students.

For a brief time, the government shut its eyes to the demonstrations in the streets and closed its ears to the people. Now, as in the case of the Philippines, democracy is an idea that has come to Korea. The irresistible force of democracy has made the immovable object of dictatorship move, and President Chun has agreed that democracy shall come to Korea.

As the cloud of tear gas thickened over Seoul in past weeks, the world reacted in support of the people of Korea. The Administration deserves credit for its effective legislative action, that left no doubt about our support for the movement to democracy in Korea.

President Chun and the chairman of the ruling party, Roh tae Woo, deserve credit for their dramatic decision in acquiescing to virtually all of the people's demands—including the holding of direct presidential elections. They have said yes to a free press, yes to respect for human rights, yes to the release of political prisoners, yes to political party activity, yes to increased local autonomy and even yes to the long overdue restoration of the civil and political rights of Kim Dae Jung.

Most of all, the people of Korea deserve credit for their courage in resisting the government's intransigence, for their determination in sustaining their peaceful protest, and for their tireless dedication in demanding a just and democratic Korea. The economic miracle of South Korea, is now about to be joined by the political miracle of South Korea. Long may Korean democracy last—and may the Olympic Games of 1988 be a fitting tribute to the great people of a great nation that is America's friends and ally in the guest for justice, human rights, and peace among all nations.

SUMMARY OF THE DEMOCRACY IN SOUTH KOREA ACT OF 1987

Senator Kennedy, Harkin, Kerry, and Mikulski introduced the Democracy in South Korea Act on June 18, 1987 in the Senate; Congressmen Foglietta, Stark and Evans, introduced comparable legislation in the House. The bill finds that the failure of the South Korean government to respect human and labor rights and to implement democratic reforms threatens the security and stability of South Korea. It also finds that the United States is violating current U.S. law by providing certain United States economic benefits to countries that do not adhere to international standards of human and labor rights.

The bill brings the U.S. into compliance with those las, and promotes basic civil, political, labor and human rights and encourages democratic reforms. To achieve these goals, the bill imposes the following conditions and requirements on U.S. policy in South Korea:

SUSPENSION OF U.S. BENEFITS ACCORDING TO CURRENT U.S. LAW:

1. *"NO" VOTE ON LOANS*—Mandates a U.S. "no" vote on multilateral development bank loans to South Korea. Section 701 of the International Financial Institutions Act requires the U.S. to oppose loans to gross violators of human rights. Despite this law, the United States has never voted against a single MDB loan to South Korea on human rights grounds but has supported $9 billion in MDB loans to Korea since 1946. In 1986, Korea received $812 million in MDB loans.

2. *DENY GSP BENEFITS*—Eliminates duty-free and preferential treatment for South Korean exports to the united States under the Generalized System of Preferences. The Trade Act of 1974 instructs the U.S. to revoke GSP status to countries that

110

violate international worker rights. Despite continued labor repression in Korea, the U.S. permitted $2.2 billion worth of Korean imports int the U.S. under GSp in 1986.

3. *DENY OPIC BENEFITS*—Prohibits the Overseas Private Investment Corporation from guaranteeing any U.S. loan or investment in Korea. The Foreign Assistance Act of 1961 prohibits the extension of such benefits to governments engaged in labor rights violations, yet the U.S. continues to provide over $270 million in such benefits to U.S. corporations in Korea.

REMOVAL OF SANCTIONS
Sanctions can be lifted only if the President certifies and the Congress approves the certification that the Government of Korea has made significant progress in:

1. Complying with internationally recognized human and labor rights.
2. Establishing a peaceful transition to democracy in Korea including:
   1. permitting political parties to organize freely;
   b. freedom of association and assembly;
   c. lifting of press restrictions;
   d. restoration of civil and political rights to individuals convicted of unlawful or improper criminal convictions;
   e. institution of basic legal reforms to ensure fair and democratic elections.

MY SUPPORT OF SENATOR KENNEDY
FOR PRESIDENT

the Daily Advance

ELIZABETH CITY, N.C. 27909, FRIDAY, OCT. 26, 1979

Kennedy may be the answer to Carter woes

To the Editor:

It is wonderful to have another Kennedy for president. Public dissatisfaction with President Carter's performance is growing daily, and Americans are looking elsewhere, most noticeably to Sen. Edward M. Kennedy of Massachusetts, for his replacement.

Sen. Kennedy is a strong public man and dynamite before an audience. No doubt, Americans realize what a mistake it made in electing Jimmy Carter.

Judging by opinion polls, Sen. Kennedy is enormously popular. President Carter's popularity reached the lowest level for any modern president. President Carter tried to pick up his slipping popularity from Vienna and Tokyo summits, a marathon domestic summit at Camp David and the subsequent departures of four cabinet members, but he did nothing to reverse the slide.

Why does President Carter keep telling the public that "Washington, D.C. has become an island and I am learning," even though he is president of the United States?

President Carter was elected in 1976 because he promised to bring new hopes and desires from the lockstep of Nixon's Watergate scandal and the falseness and blindness of the Vietnam war policy, but President Carter couldn't solve all major ills of the energy problem, unemployment, inflation, trade deficiency, devaluation of the dollar and his campaign issue of the human-rights foreign policy.

The severest human-rights violations and tortures in South Korea followed the President Carter-dictator Park summit. The Carter-Park summit was a mistake. In Seoul, photographs of President Carter and dictator Park embracing filled newspapers. The propaganda served to legitimize Park's regime and oppression.

Within six weeks of President Carter's visit, Park's court in Seoul ruled against Kim Young Sam, leader of the opposition New Democratic Party and relieved him of his chairmanship. The court proceeded to declare invalid all the appointments made by Kim. Kim Young Sam was expelled from the National Assembly by pro-Park Chung Hee's legislators which control the Chamber with the help of a large bloc of members who are not elected but appointed with Park Chung Hee's advice.

We hailed President Carter's proclaimed intention to speak out against human-rights violations anywhere in the world. We applauded President Carter's denunciation of the Kremlin's persecution of Soviet dissidents. But what about the violation of human-rights, why does President Carter's support for Park Chung Hee continue? Why has President Carter kept his silence on human rights abuses by the Park Chung Hee regime?

Right now this country is suffering with the lack of leadership. President Carter goes jogging and hugging all over the place instead of jumping on the oil companies the way John F. Kennedy handled on big steel. The oil problem should be the top national priority.

President Carter was a first President to allow foreign troops in the Western Hemisphere since President Monroe. President Carter went on national television and proved the existing Soviet combat brigade in Cuba without any appropriate action. President Carter must tell the Soviets that your troops must get out of Cuba instead of lan-ding 1,800 Marines at Guantanamo Bay Naval Base.

The Carterites are talking about a Carter-Kennedy contest as a "civil war." It was certainly a misunderstanding. Kennedy has a perfect right to challenge President Carter for the 1980 Democratic presidential nomination. It would not bring the antagonism of the North, the liberals, the Catholics and the cities against the South, the conservatives, the protestants, and the countryside. Americans are yearning for leadership regardless of the North, the South, the Catholics, the Protestants, the liberals or the conservatives.

Sen. Kennedy has his own hard work and one of the most distinguished member in the Senate. Senator Kennedy is evidently confident to bring the nation strong again. Kennedy is a man to bring the economic independence, build a new patriotism and solve the difficulties and problems of this land.

Sen. Kennedy will win, and everything will be all right.

Woo Jung Ju, Ph.D.
Professor of History
Elizabeth City State University
Elizabeth City, N.C.

United States Senate
WASHINGTON, D.C. 20510

December 27, 1979

Professor Woo Jung Ju
Dept. of History
Elizabeth City State U.
Elizabeth City, North Carolina

Dear Professor Ju:

Thank you for your comments on the shocking situation in Iran.

Our immediate priority must be to gain the safe and early release of all our fellow citizens being held hostage. The seizure of innocent Americans in our Embassy is an outrage, and I am deeply disturbed by the Iranian Government's actions in supporting this violation of all principles of international law. I absolutely oppose any submission to blackmail or intimidation.

I do not believe, however, that our indivisible support for the safe release of the hostages should lead us to condone the repressive dictatorship that existed in Iran under the Shah. To ignore the abuses of the past, in my opinion, seriously undermines our efforts to secure the freedom of the hostages. I recognized that my statements in this regard would be controversial, but I felt strongly that it was in the interest of the nation and the hostages to speak out. I opposed granting the Shah permanent asylum in this country. I welcomed Secretary Vance's assurances that no further secret decisions would be made in that direction, and I am now hopeful that the Shah's move to Panama will create a new opportunity for the Americans' safe release.

We must make two things clear to the Iranians: first, that we will not be blackmailed under any circumstances, and, second, that we are not blind to the Shah's harsh rule. I believe that this position represents our best chance to obtain the prompt freedom of all Americans held hostage in Tehran. Until the Americans are released safely, however, we must place the strongest pressure on the Iranian Government while avoiding actions that could endanger American lives.

I therefore support the Administration's decisions to terminate all oil imports from Iran, freeze the Iranian Government's assets in the United States, and cut back on Iranian diplomatic personnel. These and other appropriate actions will

115

VIRGINIA BEACH

beacon

Jan. 29/30, 1980

Iranian crisis reveals 'Carter is a coward'

From WOO JUNG JU, Ph.D.
Professor of History
Elizabeth City State University

President Carter is doing just what Richard Nixon did in 1972. His popularity reached the lowest level for any modern president up to the Iranian crisis. President Carter tried to pick up his slipping popularity from Vienna, Tokyo, and Seoul summits, a marathon domestic summit at Camp David, and subsequent departures of four cabinet members, but he did nothing to reverse the slide. The Iranian crisis resulted in President Carter's political miracle in getting a dramatic upturn in the polls.

President Carter is using the hostages to help his own re-election campaign. President Carter rejected the Iowa debate scheduled on Jan. 7, because he could not get away from Washington because of the Iranian crisis, and again refused a new debate proposed for Jan. 17 in Washington on grounds that the hostages were still in Tehran. He is a coward. Why did President Carter chose this time to let the shah enter the United States and ignore warnings from the State Department and the U.S. Embassy in Tehran? Why had President Carter placed a life of a malefactor above the lives of innocent Americans serving their country abroad? Who was the creator of the Iranian crisis? Who is the beneficiary from the crisis now?

President Carter is using the Iranian crisis for everything it's worth, but this kind of worth and unsound principle does not show strength and national unity. The Shah of Iran, criticized by Senator Kennedy and Coffin, pastor of Riverside Church in Manhattan, will be helpful to the hostages. The Carter camp's criticizing Khomeini as Hitler and Idi Amin will bring more harm to the hostages. Machiavelli said "the mass of men are very stupid and deceit is easy." I believe that leaders can deceive their subjects sometimes, but not all the time.

President Carter had asked all candidates to stay silent on the Iranian crisis and show restraint in everything but in using the Iranian crisis to freeze his political opponents.

President Carter failed to apply any real pressure to free the hostages for nearly two months, and to develop a policy that would protect American interests and prestige in the world.

President Carter failed to solve all the major ills of the energy problem, unemployment, inflation, trade deficiency, devaluation of the dollar and recession. I don't believe President Carter will do anything.

Allowing the Shah of Iran into the United States was a grave mistake. Leaders first deceived themselves and then deceived the public. The lesson written in the White House is that never again should this nation allow its presidents to have their own war and crisis.

We must restablish the Foreign Intelligence Advisory Board, a group of distinguished independent citizens reporting directly to the president on the performance and needs of intelligence agencies. No president can make any decision without the board's consent. It is time to change the Constitution and to have a one term president.

Telegram

Western Union

MSG. NO	CL. OF SVC.	PD.-COLL	CASH NO.	ACCOUNTING INFORMATION

Send the following message, subject to the terms on back hereof, which are hereby agreed to.

DATE: Feb. 29, 80 FILING TIME: 1:   A.M./P.M. SENT TIME: A.M./P.M.

☐ OVERNIGHT TELEGRAM
UNLESS BOX ABOVE IS CHECKED THIS
MESSAGE WILL BE SENT AS A TELEGRAM

TO: Senator Edward M. Kennedy CARE OF OR APT. NO.

ADDRESS & TELEPHONE NO. United States Senate

CITY — STATE & ZIP CODE Washington, D. C. 20002

New Hampshire primary showed you are going to win. God knows manufactured Iranian crisis and unfortunately innocent hostages may not come home before the November general election. President Carter has no policies for energy and inflation, and creating dangerous war atmosphere. Please guide and stand for the mankind. You will get the victory.

Woo Jung Ju, Ph.D.
Professor of History
Elizabeth City State University
Elizabeth City, N. C. 27909

SENDER'S TEL. NO.   NAME & ADDRESS

EOM

(CHG #)	(BILL TO)	(OPR #)	(HF)	(PC CODE)	(PC AMT)	(ADDRESS)	(PC AMT)	(GIFT AMT)	(TAX)	(AGT ID)	(CITY-STATE-ZIP) (CHG METH)

WESTERN UNION

FOR OPERATION COPY (SO)   X-OFF

OFFICE USE ONLY

W.U. 5210 (6/77)

117

United States Senate

WASHINGTON, D.C. 20510

March 18, 1980

Professor Woo Jung Ju
Dept. of History ·
Eliz. City State Univ.
Elizabeth City, North Carolina 27909

Dear Professor Ju:

I want you to know how deeply I appreciate your recent
letter and your expression of support for my campaign. Such
encouragement from friends around the country is a continuing
source of inspiration to me in the campaign, and I am most
grateful to you for writing to me personally.

This election is the people's chance to choose. It is their
only real opportunity to deal with the worsening condition of
their lives, and to regain control over critical issues like the
economy, energy, and foreign policy.

Over the past several months since the campaign began, I
have travelled to every region of the nation. I have found
persons like yourself deeply concerned over America's future and
our inability to deal effectively with the serious challenges
before us.

Our highest officials now admit that the economy has reached
a "crisis" stage. Yet they continue to insist their current
policies are "fine." But they are fine only for the few.

Millions of Americans are daily victims of the faltering
economy. Inflation roars ahead at 20 percent a year. The price
of energy soars. The Administration forecasts a recession in
1980 in which 1.5 million more Americans will lose their jobs --
yet they offer a federal budget that proposes to deny
unemployment compensation to the long-term unemployed.

For the elderly, inflation means cruel choices between heat
for their apartments and food on their tables. For workers, it
means harsh declines in the purchasing power of their wages. For
the poor, it means the ever deeper impoverishment of their
already bare and bleak existence. For families throughout the
land, it means dreams deferred and growing hardships in their
lives.

I believe we can deal with these challenges. In the course of this campaign, I have proposed clear and specific alternatives to the present failing policies -- alternatives that can bring our economy back to health, resolve our energy crisis, and revive our foreign policy in a way that regains the confidence of our allies and the respect of our adversaries.

Your support and encouragement will sustain me in the weeks ahead. Together, we can carry this message to the people in the primaries and caucuses to come, and in the election in the fall. And together, I am confident that we shall prevail.

Sincerely,

Edward M. Kennedy

March 18, 1980

Professor Woo Jung Ju
Dept. of History
Eliz. City State Univ.
Elizabeth City, North Carolina 27909

Dear Professor Ju:

I want you to know how deeply I appreciate your recent letter and your expression of support for my campaign. Such encouragement from friends around the country is a continuing source of inspiration to me in the campaign, and I am most grateful to you for writing to me personally.

This election is the people's chance to choose. It is their only real opportunity to deal with the worsening condition of their lives, and to regain control over critical issues like the economy, energy, and foreign policy.

Over the past several months since the campaign began, I have travelled to every region of the nation. I have found persons like yourself deeply concerned over America's future and our inability to deal effectively with the serious challenges before us.

Our highest officials now admit that the economy has reached a "crisis" stage. Yet they continue to insist their current policies are "fine." But they are fine only for the few.

Millions of Americans are daily victims of the faltering economy. Inflation roars ahead at 20 percent a year. The price of energy soars. The Administration forecasts a recession in 1980 in which 1.5 million more Americans will lose their jobs -- yet they offer a federal budget that proposes to deny unemployment compensation to the long-term unemployed.

For the elderly, inflation means cruel choices between heat for their apartments and food on their tables. For workers, it means harsh declines in the purchasing power of their wages. For the poor, it means the ever deeper impoverishment of their already bare and bleak existence. For families throughout the land, it means dreams deferred and growing hardships in their lives.

I believe we can deal with these challenges. In the course of this campaign, I have proposed clear and specific alternatives to the present failing policies -- alternatives that can bring our economy back to health, resolve our energy crisis, and revive our foreign policy in a way that regains the confidence of our allies and the respect of our adversaries.

Your support and encouragement will sustain me in the weeks ahead. Together, we can carry this message to the people in the primaries and caucuses to come, and in the election in the fall. And together, I am confident that we shall prevail.

Sincerely,

Edward M. Kennedy

March 31, 1980

Professor Woo Jung Ju
Department of History
No. Carolina University
Elizabeth City, North Carolina 27909

Dear Professor Ju:

My warm thanks for your thoughtful
congratulatory message.

I am heartened and inspired by your
encouragement and will continue to strive to bring
my message to the American people. It is urgent
that we continue to work together to meet the
challenges facing America in this critical period
of our proud history.

This is only possible with your continued
help and support, for which I am enormously
grateful.

With sincere appreciation,

Sincerely,

Edward M. Kennedy

wisconsin

Thursday, April 3, 1980

Judge not

The press' attention to Senator Edward M. Kennedy's infamous automobile accident a decade ago is unfortunate. How the press once loved the Kennedys! Why is the same press mistreating and destroying the surviving Kennedy brother?

Senator Kennedy's elder brother Joseph Kennedy was killed during a special bombing mission over Germany. President John F. Kennedy and Senator Robert Kennedy were felled by assassins' bullets. Now the last of the Kennedy brothers is being destroyed by the press.

Reporters, writers, and politicians should study neurological research results before criticizing Senator Kennedy. Head injuries and shock cause victims to fall asleep and lose any initiative and to fail to walk and talk.

In a widely reported incident, Harry Wallace of Beard's Fork, West Virginia, lost control of his car last January. The next day his car was sighted in the water by a school bus driver. It was not completely submerged, so Mr. Wallace lived to tell of his experience. He said: "I really don't remember what happened. The first thing I remember is waking up and hearing water. After failing to find a way out, I fell asleep." He was treated at the hospital for shock. No one accused him of lying or covering up.

I was injured in an automobile accident on September 26, 1979. I had minor head injuries and shock. I was treated at an emergency room. After 24 hours, I returned to the emergency room for additional treatment, but drove to to the emergency room of another hospital. A nurse couldn't find my record. I realized then that I had lost my memory.

During the 24 hours after the accident. I talked with my wife, my daughter, doctors, nurses, and police. I watched television, but I remembered nothing. I moved around without my eyeglasses for a few hours after the accident even though I am usually helpless without them. I realize now that I got severely shocked for a period after the accident.

Senator Kennedy's car lay upside down in

about eight feet of water. He escaped from the car himself, but Mary Jo Kopechne did not. Senator Kennedy dived several times to save her, but failed to do so. It is probably that Senator Kennedy did this while he was the state of shock.

How did Senator Kennedy swim across the 500 foot wide channel? In the state of shock, any person can swim. In Russia, medical scientists determined through experiments that babies a few weeks old can swim. Senator Kennedy could have moved his arms and body while the shock and reached the shore.

How could Senator Kennedy have walked to the inn, changed into dry clothes, and spoken briefly to the innkeeper? My own experience argues that anybody might talk, walk and move around while the period of shock. - Why did Senator Kennedy go to sleep and wait so long to call police? Mr. Wallace fell asleep immediately after the accident, but Senator Kennedy fell asleep hours later. I believed that I had fully recovered one day after the accident, but three days afterward, I began to worry about my injuries, car, and insurance. My full recovery occured three days after the accident. Therefore, it is impossible for Senator Kennedy to report while the shock for a period after the accident.

Senator Kennedy has suffered enough from the Chappaquiddick event. Senator Kennedy stayed out of the 1972 and 1976 presidential races because of that accident. Why does the press keep hounding him ten years later? — Woo Jung Ju, Ph. D., Professor of History, Elizabeth City State University, Elizabeth City, North Carolina, 27909.

The Daily Advance

Forum

ELIZABETH CITY, N.C., 27909, MONDAY, SEPTEMBER 8, 1980

Kennedy was the best choice

To the editor:

The Carter administration seems helpless. The world appears a more dangerous and unstable place than it was when Carter came to the White House.

His approach has never worked well internally or externally.

Inflation has doubled during the Carter administration and is now contained only by a recession bound to drive unemployment higher. The country remains heavily dependent upon foreign oil. The Soviet Union and its allies have made gains in Asia, Latin America and Africa at the expense of America. Western allies more and more are going into business in their own way. No nation and no one can stand with President Carter's policy of flip-flops and zigzags.

The United States has grown weak and has been reduced to the rank of a second-rate power by the present leadership. Carter did not take any action against Russian brigades in Cuba, and no country would ever have taken hostages from an American embassy. He failed to apply any real pressure to free the hostages for nealy 10 months and opportunized from the seizure of Americans as hostages in Iran during the primary.

President Carter should not be making deals with Moammar Khadafy, dictator of Libya, who welcomed the killers of the Israeli athletes; hijackers, and others, and fought for Idi Amin.

America should be governed by someone who understands power. Sen. Edward Kennedy is almost perfectly right on most matters of public policy and he is a politician, a cheerful, passionate and believing professional.

Kennedy is the heir to the new frontier, to the liberal tradition, to the New Deal, and he will be the symbol of desire to labor, to minorities, to progressives, and to the feeble and the elderly.

Ronald Reagan, the Republican nominee, is a conservative, so the Democratic party, the basically liberal party, should have nominated a liberal. If Sen. Kennedy were to win the presidency, he probably would be a much better president than Jimmy Carter or Ronald Reagan.

Kennedy would have quickly wiped out President Carter in the primaries, inasmuch as the polls had for years shown him as the undisputed favorite, but his presidential campaign was robbed by the manufactured hostage crisis in Iran.

Woo Jung Ju, Ph.D.
Professor of History
Elizabeth City State University

124

Moral Majority, NCPAC have wrong approach

Dear Editor:

It was very wrong to give much of the credit to the Moral Majority and the National Conservative Political Action Committee (NCPAC) for the victory of Ronald Reagan and defeat of several liberal Senators.

Dr. Norman W. Wessells, Dean, School of Humanities and Sciences, Stanford University warned against the Moral Majority and groups such as NCPAC. Dr. Wessells said that they are potentially far more dangerous than the U.S. Communist Party.

The Rev. Timothy Healy, President of Georgetown University spoke of "New Religiosity," and they are "sweeping the nation and running counter to Western religion."

Dr. A. Bartlett Giamatti, President of Yale University criticized the Moral Majority and its New Right groups as "Peddlers of coercion,"

threatening the life and the mind and the nation. Dr. Giamatti said that the Moral Majority and its clients "threaten through political pressure or public denunciation whoever dares to disagree with their authoritarian position."

Sen. Barry Goldwater, Republican's nominee for President in 1964 lashed out the Moral Majority and its satelite groups. Sen. Goldwater said that "I don't think what they're talking about is conservativism," and "I'm frankly sick and tired of the political preachers across the country telling me as a citizen that if I want to be a moral person, I must believe in A,B,C, and D. Just who do they think they are? And from where do they presume to claim the right to dictate moral beliefs to me?"

Sen Goldwater accused that "They are diverting us away from the vital issues that our government needs to address, such as national security and economic survival."

The Moral Majority and NCPAC's approaches are wrong, because our first priority is national economic survival.

I will continue to pray that the Moral Majority, NCPAC and its New Right group study more the Christian principle and soon become real Christians.

Woo Jung Ju
Elizabeth City

JUST WHEN YOU THOUGHT IT WAS SAFE TO GO BACK ON THE ROAD....

Moral Majority needs to be converted

Editor, Safety Valve:

It was very wrong to give much of the credit for the Moral Majority and the National Conservative Political Action Committee (NCPAC) which brought the victory of Ronald Reagan and defeat of several

liberal Senators. The majority of people seemed to realize that the Moral Majority and NCPAC were revealed as not speaking for all Americans, and they are really far from being a majority.

Dr. Norman K. Wessells, Dean, School of Humanities and Sciences, Stanford University warned against the Moral Majority and groups such as NCPAC. Dr. Wessells said that they are potentially far more dangerous than the U.S. Communist Party.

The Rev. Timothy Healy, President of Georgetown University spoke of "New Religiosity," and they are "sweeping the nation and run counter to Western religion."

Dr. A. Bartlett Giamatti, President of Yale University critized the Moral Majority and its New Right groups as "Pedllers of coercion," threatening the life, the mind and the nation. Dr. Giamatti said that the Moral Majority and its clients "threaten through political pressure or public denunciation whoever dares to disagree with their authoritarian position."

Sen. Barry Goldwater, Republican's nominee for president in 1964, lashed out the Moral Majority and its satellite groups. Sen. Goldwater said that "I don't think what they're talking about is conservativism, and I'm frankly sick and tired of the political preachers across the country telling me as a citizen that if I want to be a moral person, I must believe in A, B, C and D. Just who do they think they are? And from where do they presume to claim the right to dictate their moral beliefs to me?"

Sen. Goldwater accused that, "They are diverting us away from the vital issues that our government needs to address, such as national security and economic survival."

Would the Moral Majority and NCPAC take the 1 million unborn babies and feed, clothe, and educate them for 18 years? For thousands and thousands die each day from starvation. The world needs more and more monies to feed the ones already here.

The Moral Majority and NCPAC's approaches are wrong, because our first priority is national economic survival and national unity. Why all the monies the Moral Majority and NCPAC spend fighting Senator Edward M. Kennedy? Senator Kennedy stood always the symbol of desire to the labor, to unemployment, minorities, to progressiveness, and to the feeble and the elderly.

Sen. Kennedy has his own hard work and one of the most distinguished members in the Senate. Sen. Kennedy is evidently confident to bring the nation strong again. Sen. Kennedy is a man to bring the economic independence, build a new patriotism and solve the difficulties and problems of this land.

I will continue to pray that the Moral Majority, NCPAC and its New Rights group study more the Christian principle and soon become real Christians.

Woo Jung Ju, Ph.D.
Professor of History
Elizabeth City State Univ.
North Carolina

EDWARD M. KENNEDY

March 1, 1982

Dr. Woo Jung Ju
Dr. Wook Ja Ju
648 Rosaer Lane
Virginia Beach, Virginia 23462

Dear Wook Ja and Woo Jung:

It meant so much to me to have you both here for my fiftieth birthday celebration at Hickory Hill. The evening was a great success.

I also want to remind my friends who gave me such a hard time on turning 50 that the Middle Ages was followed by the Renaissance.

Seriously though, thanks for coming.

Sincerely,

[signature]

My thanks to you both

Moral dictators?

Editor, Virginian-Pilot:

The Moral Majority and the National Conservative Political Action Committee should be aware that their method of attempting to improve the morals of our nation does not coincide with the Christian doctrine.

It was very wrong to give much of the credit to the Moral Majority and NCPAC for the election victory of Ronald Reagan and the defeat of several liberal senators. The Moral Majority and NCPAC do not speak for most Americans, and they are really far from being a majority.

Sen. Barry Goldwater, Republican nominee for president in 1964, lashed out at the Moral Majority and its satellite groups. Senator Goldwater said: "I don't think what they're talking about is conservativism, and I'm frankly sick and tired of the political preachers across the country telling me as a citizen that if I want to be a moral person, I must believe in A, B, C and D. Just who do they think they are? And from where do they presume to claim the right to dictate their moral beliefs to me? They are diverting us away from the vital issues that our government needs to address, such as national security and economic survival."

Why doesn't the Moral Majority and NCPAC try to solve the major ills — the energy problem, high unemployment, inflation, trade deficiency, devaluation of the dollar, recession, rising crimes and nuclear weapons?

Would the Moral Majority and NCPAC take the million unborn babies and feed, clothe and educate them for 18 years? Thousands of people die each day from starvation.

Our first priority is national economic survival and national unity. Why are all the monies of the Moral Majority and NCPAC spent against Sen. Edward M. Kennedy? Senator Kennedy is a desirable symbol to labor, the unemployed, minorities, progressives and the feeble and the elderly.

America should be governed by someone who understands power. Senator Kennedy is almost perfectly right on most matters of public policy and he is a politician — a cheerful, passionate and believing professional.

WOO JUNG JU, Ph.D.,
Professor of History,
Elizabeth City State University,
Elizabeth City, N.C.

EDWARD M. KENNEDY
MASSACHUSETTS

United States Senate
WASHINGTON, DC 20510

January 30, 1987

Dr. Woo Jung Ju
648 Rosaer Lane
Virginia Beach, VA   23464

Dear Dr. Ju:

I thought you might like to look through the enclosed
clippings on my recent work in the new Democratic Senate!

As you will see, I began my responsibilities as Chairman of
the Labor and Human Resources Committee with a series of hearings
on national goals in health, employment, and education, which are
the key areas within the Committee's jurisdiction. It was obvious
from the hearings that realistic initiatives are available to
help us do a better job of meeting the pressing social challenges
we face.

I also intend to be active in the Senate on both the Armed
Services Committee and the Judiciary Committee. I am now
Chairman of a subcommittee on each of these committees, and I
will be making new efforts there to deal with our priorities on
defense and to resume our progress on civil rights.

It's a full plate -- and it is very satisfying to have the
opportunity to participate in setting the agenda in Congress on
these issues. Life in the Senate looks very different with our
new Democratic majority, and I hope to do my part in keeping it
that way.

With my thanks for all your help and support, and I hope that
you will find these materials of interest.

Sincerely,

Ted

The author with Senator Edward M. Kennedy

REMARKS, STATEMENTS, AND ADDRESSES OF SENATOR EDWARD M. KENNEDY

Address of Senator Edward M. Kennedy to the Democratic 1982 Mid-Term Conference, Philadelphia.

Address of Senator Edward M. Kennedy to the Democratic Mid-Term Conference.

First of all, let me reaffirm my commitment that no matter how long it may take, we shall finally write the Equal Rights Amendment into the Constitution of the United States.

Our opponents rejoice that the deadline for E.R.A. will dawn in three more days. But we reply: We have only just begun to fight. We reply: "E.R.A. won't go away."

The temporary defeat of this amendment is a national disgrace. But for us, the deadline will only be the starting line of a new crusade to pass and to ratify equal rights. Our dream still lives, and E.R.A. shall never die.

I will be proud to lead the fight in the Senate Judiciary Committee. And I will fight as well for the economic rights of women. We will demand not only equal pay for equal work, but equal pay for work of comparable worth — and not only in present jobs, but in the new occupations of our future.

We are warned that these fights will be hard. I heard the same discouraging words a year ago when we set out to sustain and strengthen the Voting Rights Act. But a week ago we crushed the filibuster of Jesse Helms and the New Right; we voted against an ancient wrong and for an abiding commitment that every citizen of any color can cast a ballot freely and have it counted fairly.

So in the cause of E.R.A. we do not worry at the fading of three more days. We are ready to spend three more years or three more decades or three more generations. As we said with civil rights, so we say with equal rights: We shall overcome some day.

We Believe In E.R.A.

And in reaching for that time, we will not rest, retreat, hesitate, equivocate or wait. We believe in E.R.A. And here in Philadelphia, where the Declaration of Independence was written, we repeat the demand that our nation at long last must hold this truth to be self-evident — that not only all men, but all people, are created equal.

So it is with every great issue that asks our best effort. The principles which have always been central to our party are at stake now as much as they have ever been before — the principles of fairness and compassion, of economic progress and social justice, of an end to discrimination against the minority of Americans who are not white, and the majority who are women. We must also pledge a society where Hispanics and all those born to the Spanish tongue will never be subjected to second-class treatment.

We meet in the midst of a fierce struggle for the shape and the soul of our generation. Last year, we were advised to be cautious and callous and uncommitted. We were told to quiet our voices, to lower our vision, and to trim our convictions to fit the fashion of a reactionary time. We were warned to say very little and to stand for even less.

But that is not the kind of Senator I have sought to be, or the kind of Democratic Party you and I have fought for. The struggle last year sometimes seemed lonely. But events since then have reaffirmed a vital truth: the last thing this nation needs in the 1980's is two Republican Parties.

As Democrats, we welcome new ideas. But we must also have the backbone to stand for our most fundamental beliefs. Faces will change; programs will succeed or fall short — but we must never become bland in our convictions or blind to the evils before us.

The women and men of our party will always think anew and act anew — for the heritage of progressives is the history of progress. But let us insist that rethinking our ideas must never be an excuse for retreating from our ideals.

We recognize that institutions are imperfect and public endeavors do have problems. But the Administration now in power has magnified those imperfections and misused those problems. They have made them a pretext for indiscriminately destroying programs — and for denying our most decent impulses toward each other.

Only last month, the President said to his fellow Republicans — and I quote: "We are the party that wants to see an America in which people can still get rich." But you and I know that the Republican road to wealth is paved with inattention and indifference. In reality, they are the party that is giving us an America where more and more people are getting poor. And that is why the people will see to it that the Republicans get the defeat they deserve in the election of 1982.

Of course, the President does say that he cares about the poor. And you know, there is one piece of evidence for that. Ronald Reagan must love poor people, because he is creating so many more of them.

Reagan's Cheeselines

We hear apologists for this Administration parrot the platitude that we cannot relive the 1960's — and obviously that is right. But it has a hollow ring, coming from those whose right-wing nostrums have brought the worst unemployment since the Great Depression, and the worst farm collapse since the Dust Bowl years. They have restored the reign of hear-nothing, see-nothing, do-nothing government. Ronald Reagan's cheese lines of

1982 are as unacceptable as Herbert Hoover's breadlines of 1932.

And let us be clear in responding to the repeated rationalization of this Administration for its failure. The President has claimed over and over that he inherited the recession when he took office. But no statistics prove that, and no economist believes it. The advisers in the White House may think they can trick the voters and shift the blame. The President should know better. And if Ronald Reagan does not know the facts about how this recession began, then Ed Meese ought to wake him up and tell him.

The President has also claimed again and again that the economy will be better tomorrow and tomorrow. He said it last year, last month, and last week. But this Administration deserves to be judged by the standard the President himself set during the 1980 campaign. We all remember the question he asked then: "Are you better off today than you were four years ago?" Now I think it is only fair to raise that question again.

Of course, a few Americans may say they are better off, because they have been privileged to enjoy million-dollar tax breaks. But I can guess what the unprivileged, unnoticed, and un-rich majority of Americans will say. You have come from them — and here at this Party Conference, you can speak for them.

Since Ronald Reagan got his job, nearly three million Americans have lost their jobs. So let me ask you: Are the working men and women of America better off today than they were two years ago?

Since this Administration was elected, the cost of home mortgages has reached the fantastic level of 18.6 percent. So let me ask you: Are the homebuyers and homebuilders of America better off today than they were two years ago?

Are Americans Better Off?

Since this Administration was elected, education, health research, and school lunches for the middle class have all been slashed. So let me ask you: Are the families of America better off today than they were two years ago?

Since this Administration was elected, they have tried three times to cut Social Security, which is "the most unkindest cut of all." So let me ask you: Are the Senior Citizens of America better off today than they were two years ago?

You can be certain that the White House will try that cut again as soon as the fall election has passed. For there is something at the heart of the Republican Party which yearns to undo Social Security.

It is the same old trick that the Republican elephant never seems to

132

forget. Republicans always pretend that they like Social Security. They said it during the 1940 campaign, not long after it passed despite their opposition. And here in Philadelphia in that year, Franklin Roosevelt gave the Democratic answer: "These same Republican leaders are all for Social Security now. They believe in it so much that they will never be happy until they can clasp it to their own chests . . . If they could only get control of Social Security, they plead, they would take so much better care of it, honest to goodness they would."

In the 1980's, we must address long-range problems in the retirement program. But we must never let this Administration savage Franklin Roosevelt's system of Social Security in order to salvage Ronald Reagan's trickle-down tax cut.

Now I have one more quotation to read and one more question to ask. Last winter, Ronald Reagan's Secretary of the Treasury said — and I quote: The economy "is going to come roaring back in the late spring." Well, spring has sprung and gone. So let me ask you: Has anyone here heard the roar?

I am tired of tough talk from reactionaries who believe in rugged individualism — if it is rugged on others and easy for themselves. Other leaders in other days have called on our best instincts as Americans. Instead, this Administration has told us to be a nation of self-seekers; in word and deed, they have summoned us to a standard of selfishness. And they have tried to hide their real purposes behind their anti-government rhetoric.

They speak of a new federalism — but their program would take the most from the truly needy; it would give states and localities more responsibilities without enough resources. In fact, their new federalism is nothing more than the old feudalism of unfeeling neglect and unforgiving laissez-faire.

There have been suggestions that Democrats should compete for a grip on the anti-government line. But much more is at stake here than a political tactic or an issue of material advantage; we face a fundamental moral test of our party and our country.

If we do not care about the immunization of the sons and daughters of American families, who will? I do not regard it as waste or fraud to banish polio and diphtheria from our homes, our schools, and our playgrounds. The real fraud is in the Administration budget. How dare they spend three million dollars a year on medicine for military pets, while they slash five million dollars from medicine for our children?

And if we do not have the decency to struggle against discrimination, then who will? We know what the other side has tried to do. And we can be proud that we have blocked their attempt to give tax exemptions for the racial prejudice of segregated schools.

Don't Burn Books

And if we do not have the wisdom to sustain public education, then who will? This is our reply to the cynical appeal of the New Right extremists: The way to support the American family is not to burn the books in our libraries, but to pay a living wage to those who teach our children how to read.

Finally, if we do not stand up for the hungry, if we do not speak up for those who work with their hands, if we do not fight on for the desperate millions of our inner cities, then who will?

If we abandon the struggle, Americans will become ever more divided from each other, living apart in separate camps of race and region, sex and class. Instead, let us as Democrats offer a different vision of America as one people, one society, one destiny, one nation where all can advance together and none are left behind.

To achieve this in the 1980's, we do not have to call ourselves neo-liberals, or cozy up to neo-conservatives. At its best, the Democratic Party has been both principled and pragmatic; we have cared both about what will work and about what is right. And I believe that in this decade, we can be true Democrats without becoming either the party of the bleeding heart or the party whose heart has turned to stone.

We can follow the vision of our future without forfeiting the values of our past. We can move forward to an economy of justice and of jobs.

New Ideas of 1980s

First, we must reverse the disastrous course of economic policy. We must state plainly that this nation cannot solve problems by throwing tax cuts at them. The Administration sold their Reagan-Kemp-Roth tax scheme as a new idea. But now we know what it really is: it is the old deal of the Republican Party in which the cards are always dealt from the bottom of the deck.

We must repeal the third year of the Reagan tax giveaway. We must revise those excessive business tax breaks and tax leasing rules which are nothing more than welfare for giant corporations.

And in this decade, Democrats will mark out the new direction of a new and simpler tax system. Real tax reform means a simple, comprehensible, broad-based, progressive tax code determined by the ability to pay a fair share — not costly, complicated, regressive tax loopholes that depend on the ability to pay a smart lawyer.

Too many Americans are now being asked to sacrifice too much. In 1982, let us insist that we shall no longer pay for the gains of the greedy with the pains of the needy. At long last, let the special interests ask what they can do for their country.

We will also shape a new industrial policy to make America more competitive in the world. Let us resolve that the economy of the United States shall never become a colony of Germany and Japan. And we will create a new partnership of business, labor and government to achieve price and wage restraint. Recession is not now — and it never has been and it never will be — our answer to inflation.

Instead of indiscriminate tax cuts, we will target incentives for productive growth. America must encourage investment in basic industry, high technology

and microchips — instead of land spe tion and slot machines.

And we will invest in people, in ht capital, not just in tools and robots will see to it that every child who ha ability will be able to afford a cc education. We will carry out a nev training plan, whose purpose is not n work — but to make individuals read productive work in the private sector will seek a new era of democracy ii workplace — and we will see to it those who work there can bargain share of profits and a say in managen

But none of this will matter unles free our economy from the tyranr high interest rates. We must stop heedless borrowing of tens of billio dollars to pay for needless corp mergers. We must stand against modern royalists who monopolize finance — and we must set aside esse credit to revive small business and f farms, and to redeem the American d of owning a home.

These are new ideas. They Democratic ideas. They turn us towa future, but they do not turn us away the greatness of our tradition as the of the people.

Old Ideas That Are Ri

. And there is something else that be said: We do not seek new ideas for the sake of their novelty. For test of an idea is not whether it is n old, but whether it is right or wrong for those old ideas which are rigl must continue a never-ending figh

I believe in the old idea of conserv and environmental protection, and ethic that can secure the natural gi this continent. I am proud that I against the confirmation of Secreta Interior James Watt — and I have for his resignation. And I am resolve America the beautiful must never be America the exploited.

I believe in the old idea of labor t to represent working men and wome must continue to demand labo reform. And we must continue to o the right wing scheme to rewrit criminal code and prosecute members for walking a picket line criminal code should be used for fig crime; it must never be misuse union-busting.

I believe in the old idea of healt as a fundamental right for every c I said it in 1978, I said it in 1980, it in 1982, and I will continue to say it comes true — if health insurance i enough for the President of the t States, the Vice President, and t members of Congress, it is good e for you and for all the people of thi

And I believe in the old idea c priorities. I support a strong na security — and needed improveme our military forces. But I will oppo Administration's indefensible incre defense spending. We cannot coun Soviet Union by bankrupting and Sc ing the American economy; we mt break the budget in order to pa military waste that weakens the n

Instead of driving auto workers off of their assembly lines and into employment lines, let us cut back the B-1 Bomber, which is nothing more than a supersonic Edsel in the sky.

Instead of cutting off food stamps, let us cut back the feast of military aid to fatten dictatorships around the world. Let us use our full influence to respond to the plea for liberty, whether it comes from the campesinos in Latin America, the refuseniks in Moscow, or the members of the Solidarity Union imprisoned in Poland. I had my disagreements with the last Administration. But on the vital issue of human rights, Ronald Reagan is wrong — and Jimmy Carter was right.

The Nuclear Freeze

Finally, in seeking the oldest human dream of peace on earth, we can be proud that our Party stands for the most important new idea of all. We stand for an immediate, comprehensive, bilateral, nuclear weapons freeze between the United States and the Soviet Union. A freeze on the mounting total of nuclear megadeath can bring us back from the brink of humanity's third and last world war.

I reject the Administration's loose talk about firing a nuclear warning shot during a European crisis. They have no right to make that nuclear gamble. There is no such thing as a limited nuclear war.

Now the President and his advisers are demanding more and more money for civil defense. They are discussing the evacuation of our major cities — which would require a week's advance warning of an impending attack and which would surely tempt the Soviets to a preemptive strike. What are the Russians supposed to think if their spy satellites see streams of cars leaving Philadelphia, clogging the bridges across the Delaware River, crawling along highways toward the sand dunes and summer cottages of the New Jersey shoreline?

But there is no sanctuary on the beach. I wish the Reagan Administration would spend less time preparing for a nuclear war and more time preventing one.

Together, the two great powers now possess the equivalent of one million Hiroshima bombs. Our stockpiles equal four tons of T.N.T. for every man, woman, and child presently living on this planet. Our arsenals are bristling with weapons that could kill more people, burn more buildings, and sack more cities, than in all the conflicts from the beginning of history. Despite all our bombs and all our missiles, we stand essentially defenseless upon a stage on which the human drama could be closed in the flashing of a fireball.

The Democratic Party must never yield on the issue of the nuclear freeze. Let us resolve that this atomic age shall not be succeeded by a second stone age. Let us work to make the world safe for human survival. And let us say that if the government cannot control nuclear arms, then people must change the government.

In closing, let me say something to all of you who are here, no matter what side you were on in the primaries of 1980. South and North, West and East, the enduring principles that now unite us as Democrats are stronger than any political differences that may ever divide us again.

So let this be our pledge — that we will be, as we have been before and at our best, an advocate for the average man and woman, a voice for the voiceless, a partisan for people who suffer and are weak, a source of excellence and a witness to the belief that America can still do better.

Struggle Has Made Us Stronger

In striving for that ideal, we have had our scars and our sorrows, our failures and our fears. We have made our share of mistakes and we have felt the sting of defeat. But we have stood our ground and the struggle has made us stronger.

We have heard it said that we were out of style. But let it also be said of us that we were never without conscience or conviction — that we did not lose our sense of perspective — or our sense of humor.

We have refused to bend with the wind or break with the waves. We have declined to be neutral or equivocal. For we have seen the pain of people in every part of our land who have lost far more than we. We see that a Democratic Party which is truly Democratic has never been more needed in our generation.

And so now we can look forward to our chance, in the words of Tennyson, to:

Ring out . . . the ancient forms of party
    strife . . .
Ring out . . . the faithless coldness of
    the times . . .
Ring out the thousand wars of old,
Ring in the thousand years of peace!
Ring in . . . the larger heart, the kindlier
    hand;
Ring out the darkness of the land.

Only a few months ago, Democrats were scorned and told that our day was done. But now we know and all America knows that for us as Democrats, and for those who have always looked to us for help and hope, the dawn is near, our hearts are bright, our cause is right, and our day is coming again.

➤"

134

STATEMENT OF SENATOR EDWARD M. KENNEDY
ON MIDDLE EAST TRIP
BOSTON, MASSACHUSETTS
DECEMBER 20, 1986

I have just returned from a seven-day visit to the Middle East, during which I traveled to Israel, Jordan and Egypt. In the course of this trip, I met with the head of state, the prime minister, the foreign minister and the defense minister of each of these countries.

I returned to the United States with serious concerns about the future of American involvement in this dangerous and volatile area of the world. The Iranian arms sale has done enormous damage to our interests in the Middle East. At best, the United States is viewed as inconsistent, naive, confused and incompetent. At worst, the United States is seen as deceptive, disloyal, erratic and unreliable.

The peace process in the Middle East is dead in the water. The lack of any serious diplomatic initiative by the United States has been compounded by the secret and erratic machinations of the past eighteen months. One of the gravest threats to peace that Israel faces today is not from guns or tanks or terrorists, but from the appearance that America is no longer a serious participant in the high-stakes diplomacy in the region.

Both our Israeli and our Arab friends in the Middle East are deeply concerned about the spread of Islamic fundamentalism from Iran throughout the Arab world, and about the increased incidence of terrorism by radical groups. Our decision to sell arms to Iran in exchange for hostages, intensifies their concerns on both counts. It is seen as an effort to curry favor with the most dangerous forces in the region, with those who work up destabilize moderate regimes, and with those who continue to export terrorism as in instrument of national policy. The decision is also seen as providing support to Khomeini in the Iran-Iraq War and as demonstrating to the terrorists that their terrorism—murder and kidnapping—pays off.

The need is urgent for the United States to regain its standing as a strong and indispensable participant in the vents of the Middle East. What is most required at this difficult time is bold, imaginative and vigorous diplomacy to review the peace process.

We must recommit ourselves to United Nations Resolutions 242 and 338, and offer our assistance in every feasible way to encourage the Arab nations to pursue peace with Israel—directly and at the negotiating table. As a preliminary step toward this goal, I urge the Administration to appoint a U.S. special envoy to the Middle East, to repair the damage from the Iranian arms deal, and to demonstrate the urgency of America's efforts to revive the stalled peace process.

High level U.S. delegations have rushed to Europe in recent weeks to reassure our NATO allies about the stability and goals of American foreign policy—and we should do no less for the cause of peace in the Middle East.

Finally, while these important efforts are underway, I also urge the Administration to agree with a three-/or fourfold increase in our current minimal commitment of approximately seven million dollars in U.S. foreign assistance funds for development programs in the West Bank in the present fiscal year. Such assistance has the full support of the Government of Israel and the Government of Jordan; it is the best means to reduce the levels of violence and terrorism, and to improve the daily lives of the people who are most victimized by the continuing current crisis. The debacle over Iran benefits no one but the terrorists, and we have no time to love in regaining the initiative.

OPENING STATEMENT OF SENATOR
EDWARD M. KENNEDY
HEARINGS BY THE SENATE COMMITTEE ON LABOR
AND HUMAN RESOURCES
NATIONAL GOALS IN HEALTH, EMPLOYMENT AND
EDUCATION
JANUARY 12, 1987

This is a new Congress, and it marks the beginning of a new era. For several years, the nation has been engaged in a period of retrenchment that has left serious scars on our society. I believe that the worst is over, and that the nation once again senses its own powers and possibilities—that American is again ready to move ahead.

After years of ignoring and fleeing difficult national problems, the country is ready to take stock of where we are, to compare our performance with other nations, to measure ourselves against our ideals—and to act accordingly.

These hearings will assess where we stand—and where we should be heading. In stating facts plainly, I do not intent to indict the past, but to touch a higher instinct, the sense we have always had at our greatest moments in the past, the belief that America can do better—better than we are now doing, and better than others can do. Americans are ready to face up to the real State of the Union, and to resume the challenge of building this country, a job that is never done. There hearings are not a partisan effort to highlight weaknesses, but a shared undertaking to rebuild national strengths.

We cannot be complacent, when America ranks 17th in the world in infant mortality, barely ahead of Cuba. We cannot be satisfied when America ranks 4th in the world of literacy. We cannot rest on any laurels, when America is 81st in the world in economic growth, when our students are outperformed by their counterparts in other countries, when our quality of life is below that of most Western European countries. At the present rate, the standard of living in West Germany in 25 years will be twice

137

as high as ours. I say, the centennial Congress must not acquiesce in the continuing decline in the American century.

We must also measure ourselves against our own past. The average 30-year-old American male earns 10 percent less in real terms than his father earned at the same age. The average American family earns less than it did in 1973. We cannot accept a future in which America is constantly losing ground against its past. We will not settle for a tomorrow in which we become a lesser people in a lesser land.

No cause is closer to my heart than quality health care for all citizens. As we begin the 100th Congress, this ideal is threatened by complex challenges. But we also stand on the threshold of immense opportunities.

Thirty-seven million fellow citizens—including more than eleven million children—lack basic health insurance. Millions of senior citizens, despite the promise of Medicare, are vulnerable to the high cost of catastrophic illness. Dread diseases—including the worldwide epidemic of AIDS—threaten the life and health of every American.

But these problems are also opportunities. A new consensus is emerging to assure that every citizen has access to the essential health care that constitutes simple justice. Secretary of Health and Human Services Otis Bowen has already provided courageous and impressive leadership toward the goal of catastrophic health insurance for elderly Americans. The miracles of modern medical research and biotechnology offer hope for cures to afflictions as different and as devastating as cancer, AIDS, and schizophrenia. A national commitment to health promotion and disease prevention can bring the blessings of decent health to millions who would otherwise suffer from our neglect. But none of these opportunities can be realized without national leadership, public commitment, clear understanding, and sound proposals.

The witnesses at today's hearing on National Goals in Health will include distinguished experts who will help diagnose the maladies and suggest solutions—and ordinary citizens who will bear witness to the personal suffering that could be avoided by wiser policy.

If we meet these challenges and take responsible steps to improve the quality of health care, the 100th Congress can be the best Congress on health care since the enactment of Medicare and Medicaid two decades ago.

The key issues at the top of my agenda include:
— Access to reasonably priced health insurance for every citizen.
— Protection for senior citizens against the financial burden of catastrophic illness.
— Improved health care for children, especially the newborn.
— Enhanced biomedical research.
— A new priority for health promotion and disease prevention.

The state of employment in America deserves equally vigorous attention, and that will be the subject of tomorrow's hearing. Some paint a rosy portrait of economic recovery, but the true scene is far different. Millions of Americans are out of work; whole regions of the country and whole sectors of the economy are in recession; high-wage manufacturing jobs are disappearing at an alarming rate; low-wage jobs are proliferating in their place.

Since the recession of 1981, the unemployment rate has hovered around 7 percent. In all the years between the Great Depression and 1980, the jobless rate reached that high level only twice. We are enduring the unique phenomenon today of recession levels of unemployment at a time of supposed recovery.

This staggering unemployment inflicts enormous damage on our society. Every man, woman and child in America would be $11,000 richer if the unemployment rate had average 5.8 percent over the past ten years instead of 7 percent. And this loss does not include the human costs of the increased crime, the mental and physical illness, the divorce and suicide that accompany chronic high unemployment.

But unemployment is only one facet of our concern about the workplace. The destruction of manufacturing jobs and the rise of service jobs pose a threat to our economic future. A recent study for the Joint Economic Committee finds that nearly 6 out of 10 wage earners hold jobs paying $7,000 a year or less. All of the increased employment since 1979 has been realized by jobs which pay less than the median wage in 1973. If this widening gap between high-wage and low-wage employment persists, the standard of living of workers will fall, and the cherished principle of progress will fail.

Ideologies such as laissez-faire and survival of the fittest are not adequate responses to these festering needs. They pose major unmet challenges for our nation's leadership. We know how to reduce unemployment, and to preserve and create good jobs for American workers. But to do so requires a commitment to recog-

139

nize trends honestly—and to correct them quickly.

In education, there is just as much to do, and that will be the subject of Wednesday's hearing. The recent study on illiteracy by the National Assessment of Educational Progress shows how poorly much of our population is faring in the basic skills needed of people are to develop themselves, support themselves, and participate in society.

The economic battles of tomorrow are being fought in the classrooms of today. But too many of our children are being disarmed unilaterally by educational policies and budget dogmas that are anti-student, anti-opportunity and anti-future. The prospects are bleakest for the children most neglected in recent years. School systems and educational institutions may be restored to their former stature, but the children whose lives have been stunted by these years of neglect may never be restored to their full potential.

We must ask not only what resources we need, but how to extract the most from those resources. We must seek ways to stretch education funds, so that every dollar spent is used effectively. We must pursue principles which reward school districts for meeting improvement goals. We must adopt programs which combine federal dollars with funds from states, localities, and private industry in order to stretch our resources as far as possible. Through satellite technology, we can make a wealth of rich new educational possibilities available to pupils whose horizons are limited by schools too poor or too remote to provide them.

It is not enough to stand still, look back, sell the family jewels, and hope for the best. Just as the darkness reminds us of the light, remembering things past is most useful when it reminds us of our ability to meet and master challenges. In the end, the challenge is neither partisan nor new. Theodore Roosevelt called on America to "Look up, not down; look out, not in; look forward, not back; the lend a hand."

I hope that these hearings will remind us not just of where we stand, but of what we stand for. Full employment for our workers, compassion for our needy, first-class education for our children, quality health care and equal opportunity for all Americans are not a dying dream. With better and wiser strategies, we can bring the real America closer to the great goals for which America has always stood.

I look forward to working in Congress and with the Administration in a new spirit of initiative and action to deal with these essential items on the unfinished agenda of America.

140

REMARKS OF SENATOR EDWARD M. KENNEDY
STATE HOUSE CONFERENCE
BRINGING DOWN THE BARRIERS TO OPPORTUNITY
BOSTON
JANUARY 17, 1987

I want to thank the Governor for that kind introduction, and I'm delighted to have the privilege of addressing this distinguished conference. Coming here this morning reminds me once again how proud I am to be from Massachusetts and to have the privilege of serving our Commonwealth in Washington.

It would have been easy for Governor Dukakis to arrange this conference to showcase our extraordinary economic achievements in Massachusetts, because we're proud of them and proud of his leadership. But it is even more fitting for this conference to concentrate on our unmet needs, and on how much remains to be done to realize the time-honored Massachusetts dream of becoming a shining city upon a hill. For the barriers we face do not just apply to others. They are barriers we all confront in the unending American struggle to create a more just and open society.

So I am honored to be here—and even more honored to tell you that the new Democratic majority in Congress is in place, at work, and ready to move ahead. Earlier this week, the Senate Labor and Human Resources Committee began a series of hearings on national goals in the three key areas of our jurisdiction—health, employment, and education. The message from dozens of witnesses in each area and from all walks of life are striking. They painted a distressing picture of unacceptable coexistence in contemporary America—extraordinary opportunity co-existing side-by-side with extreme deprivation.

We heard that the economy has generated record levels of employment—but does not provide even a poverty level standard of living for 30 billion citizens. We learned that the labor market has arms for high school and college graduates—but that record numbers of drop-outs are swelling the ranks of adult illiterates. We were told that before the end of this century, most workers will be women—but that one out of every ten American women between the ages of 15 and 19 will bear a child this year. We found that health care will consume nearly twelve percent of our gross national product next year—but that 37 million Americans, including 11 million children, lack adequate health insurance and access to basic care. And we learned that the direct economic costs of drug and alcohol abuse will reach ten percent of the federal budget next year, without even counting the billions more paid in human suffering.

To understand these numbers is to chart our path for the years ahead. The immovable object of Reaganism is about to meet the irresistible force of human need. And the clash will involve all of us—Governors and Mayors, Senators and Representatives, select women and men, educators and workers, business and professional leaders.

Through the leadership of a committed governor and the skills of a dedicated staff, ET has brought jobs and hope to those on welfare and became a model for the nation. But as we learned together here, money and a good idea were not enough to pull the program through. Business leaders did their part by ensuring that the promise of jobs was followed by the reality of work. And over 30,000 successful ET graduates did their part too—by accepting a risk and seeing the challenge through. That is what partnership is all about—public an private, we need each other and we succeed together.

That model is available for progress on many other issues. No democracy and no free society can long accept a pattern of growing injustice and inequality. To stand in place is to fall behind. To deny the dream of equal opportunity is to invite the nightmare of Howard Beach.

In recent years, we have heard a President claim that America was back and standing tall. But the claim was false. Anyone can seem tall when they are standing on the barriers. The true test whether America is standing tall is whether we are joining to tear the barriers down. Opportunity in America must exist for all, not just for the few with wealth and power and access bought with their special interest campaign contributions.

As Chairman of the Labor and Human Resources Committee

in the Senate, I intend to see that we do all we can to reduce the barriers to opportunity that plague each of the key areas of our jurisdiction. Our years in the Reagan wilderness are over. The time has come to set a new agenda of social progress for America, and I am proud to represent a Commonwealth that has done so much to lay the groundwork for that agenda.

Too many of our fellow citizens, victimized by hunger and disease, are denied the chance to become productive citizens. We must assure access to reasonably priced health insurance for every citizen, and protect every senior citizen against the burden of catastrophic disease. No elderly American should have the fear of serious illness compounded by the fear of financial ruin for his family.

The dismal state of employment in America deserves equally vigorous attention. Some paint a rosy portrait of recovery, but the honest picture is far different. Millions of Americans are out of work, out of luck, and out of hope. Whole regions of the country are in depression, and whole sectors of the economy are in recession. High-wage manufacturing jobs are disappearing at an alarming rate, and low-wage jobs are proliferating in their place.

Since 1981, the unemployment rate has hovered around seven percent. In all the years between the Great Depression and 1980, the jobless rate reached that level only twice. I say, we can do a better job on jobs than to subject this wealthy land to recession levels of unemployment at a time of supposed economic recovery. Every man, woman, and child in America would be $11,000 richer today if the unemployment rate had averaged 5.8 percent over the past ten years instead of seven percent. And this loss does not include the human costs of increased crime, mental and physical illness, divorce and suicide that are the accomplices of chronic high unemployment.

The destruction of manufacturing jobs and the rise of service jobs pose an equally dangerous threat to our economic future. The Reagan Administration boats about its record on job creation. But a recent study for the Joint Economic Committee found that six out of ten jobs created in the past six years pay $7,000 a year or less. All of the increased employment since 1979 has been realized by jobs paying less than the median wage in 1973. If the spreading gap between high and low-wage employment persists, the standard of living of all workers will fail, and the cherished principle of progress will fail. Ideologies such as laissez-faire, let them eat

143

cake, and survival of the fittest are not adequate responses to these festering needs. We know how to reduce unemployment, to preserve good jobs, and to create worthwhile new jobs for American workers. But to do so requires a commitment to recognize trends honestly—and correct them quickly.

In education, there is just as much to do. The recent study on illiteracy by the National Association of Educational Progress shows how poorly our population is faring in the basic skills needed for people to develop themselves, support themselves, and contribute to society.

The economic battles of tomorrow are being fought in the classrooms of today. But too many of our children are being unilaterally disarmed by educational ideologies and budget dogmas that are anti-student, anti-opportunity and anti-future. The prospects are bleakest for the pupils most neglected in recent years. School systems and educational institutions may be restored to their former stature. But the children whose lives have been stunted by these intervening and destructive years of neglect may never regain their full potential—and that loss is a waste in which America should never have acquiesced.

We must ask not only what resources we need, but how to extract the most from those resources. We must seek ways to stretch education funds, so that dollars spent are used effectively. We must pursue principles which reward school districts for meeting improvement goals. We must adopt programs which combine federal dollars with fund from states, localities, and private industry to extend our resources as far as possible.

Through satellite technology, we can provide a wealth of rich new educational possibilities to pupils whose horizons are limited by schools too poor or too remote to provide them. Here, our Commonwealth leads the way. MCET, the Massachusetts Corporation for Educational Telecommunications, has launched the first regional project to make the best of our teachers available to all of New England. Some would give priority to Star Wars as the way to our national interest. But I reply, Star Schools are the true path to our national future.

Finally, we must learn to pay for what we need. I voted for Gramm-Rudman-Hollings in the past and I would vote for it again today—because America must learn to live within its means. I am convinced that new approaches can work without increased spending. I recognize the restrictions of the present budget—and

144

I welcome the challenge to do more within those constraints.

I shall not hesitate to recommend new programs that are needed—and I shall not hesitate to recommend the elimination of old programs that have failed. America does not have to spend more to do more.

It is not enough to stand still, look back, sell the family jewels, and hope for the best. In the end, the challenge is neither partisan nor new. John F. Kennedy taught us how to get America moving. Theodore Roosevelt called on America to "Look up, not down; look out, not in; look forward, not back; and lend a hand."

The tasks are formidable, and in many states, the initiative in recent years has passed to state and local governments and to those demands and are rightly basking in the local success and national acclaim that our welfare and jobs program has received. And as a Celtics fan, let me say that if Mike Dukakis slam dunks the Democratic caucuses and primaries a year from now, the record books will give an assist to a tiny little character from outer space named ET.

Whatever the future may hold for our friend and Governor, a new awakening is stirring in America, and I am proud to join with all of you in the grand undertaking that lies ahead.

REMARKS OF EDWARD M. KENNEDY
MARTIN LUTHER KING, JR. HOLIDAY
UNION UNITED METHODIST CHURCH
JANUARY 18, 1987

First, let me thank Reverend Stith for that warm introduction.

Two decades ago, the dreamer we honor this morning asked his own congregation to remember him as a drum major for justice, a drum major for peace, a drum major for righteousness. Today, the community of Boston, and especially this church, are blessed because Charles Stith is our drum major. Through his work, the dream of Dr. King of racial justice and full civil rights still lives. By his minister, Reverend Stith is bringing all of us closer to the day when Dr. King's great dream finally comes true for our city, our Commonwealth, and our country.

At the historic March on Washington a quarter century ago, Martin Luther King stood before a quarter million people assembled at the memorial to our greatest Republican President. And on that famous day, Dr. King, heir of Abraham Lincoln, addressed the crowd in these words:

We have come t our nation's Capitol to cash a check. When the architects of our republic wrote the magnificent words of the Constitution and the Declaration of Independence, they were signing a promissory note to which every American was to fall heir. This note was a promise that all men would be guaranteed the unalienable rights of life, liberty, and the pursuit f happiness.

In the Declaration of Independence, the Constitution, and the Bill of Rights, America's first patriots established a society based on the goals of liberty and justice for all. The founders were not perfect, just as we are not perfect today. But the genius they bequeathed to us was a form of government based on opportunity. In the 200 years since then, we have surpassed their aspirations beyond human measure and created a nation of unparalleled power and influence. But measured against the promise of America, we have also fallen short in ways that continue to plague us and divide us. It is a national tragedy and a national disgrace that after 200 years of progress, the goal of racial justice now seems to be receding, not advancing.

After 200 years, there is justice in health care, when a newborn baby who is black is twice as likely to die in the first year of life as a baby who is white? After 200 years, where is justice in education, when the doors to our colleges and universities are being closed and locked against minorities, when student aid is being slashed, and when campuses even in our own Commonwealth are becoming battlegrounds of racism instead of peaceful avenues to understanding? After 200 years, where is economic justice, when black Americans are condemned to the bottom of the pay scale, and government abandons its commitment to affirmative action in employment? After 200 years, where is justice in democracy, when intransigent public officials who fear the power of the black vote, speak with tongues of hypocrisy about ballot security, and conspire to prevent black citizens from casting their votes on election day?

The check of which Dr. King spoke—the check for liberty and equality—was drawn on a bank account whose funds have been withdrawn by a national Administration that speaks platitudes about doing better but persists in doing worse.

The bankrupt policies of the Reagan Administration have spawned a national environment that encourages discrimination and repudiates opportunity. The decade of the 1980's has borne witness to an unconscionable retreat from the steady advances in civil rights that have always been one of the highest measures of our progress as a nation. The proud independence of the Civil Rights Commission has been dismantled and destroyed, the open-minded idealistic leaders on the Commission have been replaced by ideologues whose narrow-minded concerns are the antithesis of civil rights. Even the extension of the Voting Rights Act was jeopardized, in spite of the overwhelming evidence that minorities are still denied the constitutional right to vote for the candidate of their choice.

The Department of Justice has become an anti-justice department. It has actively sought to terminate court decrees requiring affirmative action in employment, and it has encouraged white employees to oppose affirmative action policies. Candidates with demonstrated records of racial insensitivity or even outright hostility have been nominated as federal judges, including even the Chief Justice of the United States.

This abstract retreat on civil rights at the highest levels of government has exacted a high price. Minority citizens have become targets of convenience for the fears and frustrations of other Americans seeking their own education, their own employment, their own economic security. I say to you, we must categorically reject the insidious philosophy of this Administration, that "If you are white, everything will be all right; but if you are black—get back."

That attitude has spawned incidents of racism that would have been unthinkable ten years ago. The life of a young black man is lost to the sudden violence of white teenagers in Howard Beach. A black student at The Citadel is threatened by white cadets dressed as Ku Klux Klansmen. A white man in Kansas City, Missouri, attempts to force a black family to move from the neighborhood by attacking their home five times with guns and explosives. And here at home, at the University of Massachusetts at Amherst, white students respond to the World Series loss of the Red Sox by attacking fellow black students who cheered for the Mets. And you and I know why they cheered for the Mets.

These are not just isolated cases of violence and bigotry. As Dr. King taught us, "Injustice anywhere is a threat to justice everywhere." Racism feeds on itself. Each time an individual's rights are violated, it becomes easier the next time for others to lose their rights as well. Bad as they are, the episodes of racism that mar the American landscape today are nurturing worse incidents tomorrow.

There are those who counsel us to be silent in this reactionary time, to look the other way, and to hope for the best. But I refuse to stand mute when liberty is denied and justice is deferred. I reject the advice of those who say civil rights can wait until 1988, and that it is better politics today to neglect human needs. For the landscape I see has not been entirely barren over the past six years. Each individual can make a difference—and some of us have tried. As my brother Robert Kennedy told the students at Capetown in South Africa in 1966:

Each time a person stands up for an ideal, or acts to improve the lot of others, or strikes out against injustice, he sends forth a tiny ripple of hope, and crossing each other from a million different centers of energy and daring, those ripples build a current that can sweep down the mightiest walls to oppression and resistance.

I am proud to stand here today as the sponsor of the Martin Luther King Holiday Bill, the sponsor of the Voting Rights Act, and the sponsor of Fair Housing. I am proud to speak for legal services for the poor, for school integration, and for the integrity of the federal courts. I am proud to be the sponsor in this Congress of the District of Columbia Statehood Bill and the Equal Rights Amendment to the Constitution. And I am proud to have sponsored the law in the last Congress that established economic sanctions against the Government of South Africa, over the veto of the President.

In ways such as these, on the issue of full human liberty for the minority of Americans who are not white and the majority who are women, I will never give up and I will never give in. When the timid say they fear even to try anymore, we reply that we still have a shining, powerful dream. When we hear a new version of the old refrain that speaks of gradualism, we reply: "What about Americanism?" And when we are told to wait for tomorrow and tomorrow and tomorrow, for the next election or the next generation, we reply, in the words of Martin Luther King from the Birmingham Jail: "now is the time."

I say to you, now is the time—now is always the time—to commit ourselves to the dream of Dr. King.

I ask you, when is the time for the right of every person who is able and willing to work to have a decent job? You and I know the answer: Now is the time. When is the time for the right of every young person to a decent education? Now is the time. When is the time for the right of every man, woman, and child in America to decent housing and decent health care? Now is the time. When is the time to end apartheid in South Africa? Now is the time. And finally, when is the time for the right of even the least among us to rise from the shadow of poverty into the sunshine of liberty? Now is the time.

We need national leadership that is more committed to rights such as these in our own land and to full human rights around the world. We must understand that our national interest demands progress and justice for every citizen in America, and that our national ideals demand closer relations with the people of black Africa—not constructive engagement with the apartheid regime of white South Africa.

We know that the path ahead will not be easy. Change and progress never are. But now is the time—and today is the day—to reaffirm the goals of Martin Luther King and make them our own. May his vision be our vision, his strength our strength, his struggle our struggle. In the words of Dr. King's great letter in 1963 to his fellow clergymen,

> Let us all hope that the dark clouds of racial prejudice will soon pass away, that the deep fog of misunderstanding will be lifted from our fear-drenched communities, and that in some not-too-distant tomorrow, the radiant stars of love and brotherhood will shine over our great nation with all of their scintillating beauty.

That is our prayer too in 1987, on this 58th anniversary of his birth. And with God as our guide, may we have the wisdom and the courage to carry on his work, so that at long last we shall be able to rise together and say with him, "Free at last, free at last, thank God Almighty, we are free at last!"

DISAPPEARANCE OF THE
MILITARY DICTATORSHIP

J. W. FULBRIGHT, ARK., CHAIRMAN

JOHN SPARKMAN, ALA.   ALEXANDER WILEY, WIS.
HUBERT H. HUMPHREY, MINN.   BOURKE B. HICKENLOOPER, IOWA
MIKE MANSFIELD, MONT.   GEORGE D. AIKEN, VT.
WAYNE MORSE, OREG.   HOMER E. CAPEHART, IND.
RUSSELL B. LONG, LA.   FRANK CARLSON, KANS.
ALBERT GORE, TENN.   JOHN J. WILLIAMS, DEL.
FRANK J. LAUSCHE, OHIO
FRANK CHURCH, IDAHO
STUART SYMINGTON, MO.
THOMAS J. DODD, CONN.

CARL MARCY, CHIEF OF STAFF
DARRELL ST. CLAIRE, CLERK

United States Senate

COMMITTEE ON FOREIGN RELATIONS

Augugs 17, 1961

Mr. Woo Jung Ju
Box 3013 E.T. Station
Commerce, Texas

Dear Mr. Ju:

     As a member of the Foreign Relations Committee, I
was most pleased to receive your letter concerning America's
foreign policy. I appreciated receiving your views, and you
can be assured I will keep them in mind in the months ahead.

     With all good wishes.

     Sincerely,

Hubert H. Humphrey

United States Senate
Minority Leader

August 21, 1961

Mr. Woo Jung Ju
Box 3013 E. T. Station
Commerce, Texas

Dear Mr. Ju:

I examined your letter of August 6 with a great deal of interest. I am quite sure that if the devotion of the Korean people to sound democratic principles is not impaired that democracy will not die in Korea. To be sure, she is having her problems but some of these no doubt spring from the necessary adjustments which must be made after the terrible ordeal which beset Korea so long.

Sincerely,

Everett McKinley Dirksen

CLINTON P. ANDERSON, N. MEX., CHAIRMAN

RICHARD B. RUSSELL, GA.   MARGARET CHASE SMITH, MAINE
WARREN G. MAGNUSON, WASH.   CLIFFORD P. CASE, N.J.
STUART SYMINGTON, MO.   BOURKE B. HICKENLOOPER, IOWA
JOHN STENNIS, MISS.   CARL T. CURTIS, NEBR.
STEPHEN M. YOUNG, OHIO   KENNETH B. KEATING, N.Y.
THOMAS J. DODD, CONN.
HOWARD W. CANNON, NEV.
SPESSARD L. HOLLAND, FLA.
J. HOWARD EDMONDSON, OKLA.

EVERARD H. SMITH, JR., CHIEF COUNSEL

United States Senate

COMMITTEE ON
AERONAUTICAL AND SPACE SCIENCES

April 22, 1963

Mr. Woo Jung Ju
University of Oklahoma
Norman, Oklahoma

Dear Woo Jung:

  I am happy to acknowledge your letter
in which you have expressed your views on the
present situation in South Korea.

  I want you to know that I share your
interest and concern in this matter, as I know
many other Americans do. I am going to ask the
Department of State to give me a report on the
latest developments in South Korea, and I will
be in touch with you as soon as I have received
this information.

Sincerely yours,

J. Howard Edmondson

154

CLINTON P. ANDERSON, N. MEX., CHAIRMAN

RD B. RUSSELL, GA.   MARGARET CHASE SMITH, MAINE
EN G. MAGNUSON, WASH.   CLIFFORD P. CASE, N.J.
RT SYMINGTON, MO.   BOURKE B. HICKENLOOPER, IOWA
STENNIS, MISS.   CARL T. CURTIS, NEBR.
HEN M. YOUNG, OHIO   KENNETH B. KEATING, N.Y.
AS J. DODD, CONN.
RB W. CANNON, NEV.
GARD L. HOLLAND, FLA.
WARD EDMONDSON, OKLA.

EVERARD H. SMITH, JR., CHIEF COUNSEL

United States Senate

COMMITTEE ON
AERONAUTICAL AND SPACE SCIENCES

May 9, 1963

Mr. Woo Jung Ju
University of Oklahoma
Norman, Oklahoma

Dear Woo Jung:

You will recall that in my
letter of April 22 I stated I was asking the
Department of State to give me a report on
the latest development in South Korea.

I have just received a reply from
Assistant Secretary of State Frederick G.
Dutton and I am enclosing a copy of his letter
for you. I hope that the information Assistant
Secretary Dutton has outlined in his letter
will be satisfactory to you.

Sincerely yours,

J. Howard Edmondson

WESTERN UNION TELEGRAM

W. P. MARSHALL, PRESIDENT

1207 (4-55)

NO. WDS.-CL. OF SVC.	PD. OR COLL.	CASH NO.	CHARGE TO THE ACCOUNT OF	TIME FILED
54 DL	PD	ENGELILE MISS		

Send the following message, subject to the terms on back hereof, which are hereby agreed to

To LYNDON B JOHNSON, PRESIDENT

Street and No. WHITE HOUSE

Care of or Apt. No.

Destination WASHDC

'1935 APR 17 AM 11 07 19.

I AM UNDERSTANDING YOURS REFUSAL MY REQUEST, DATED MARCH 5, 1965.

PLEASE CANCEL YOUR OFFICIAL INVITATION GENERAL PARK CHUNG-HEE.

PRESIDENT, REPUBLIC OF KOREA. MR PARK HAS NO AUTHORITY TO SPEAK

FOR THE KOREAN PEOPLE. DONT REPEAT THEODORE ROOSEVELT'S POLICY

TO KOREA. YOU SEE WHAT HAPPENING IN KOREA NOW.

WOO JUNG JU
BOX 1185
STATE COLLEGE MISS

Sender's name and address (For reference)

Sender's telephone number

156

NO. WDS.-CL. OF SVC. | PD. OR COLL. | CASH NO. | CHARGE TO THE ACCOUNT OF

OVER NIGHT TELEGRAM

UNLESS BOX ABOVE IS CHECKED THIS MESSAGE WILL BE SENT AS A TELEGRAM

1969 AUG 10 PM 6 17

Send the following message, subject to the terms on back hereof, which are hereby agreed to

TO   Richard M. Nixon, President of the U.S.

CARE OF OR AVT. NO.

STREET & NO.   Summer White House

TELEPHONE

CITY & STATE   San Clemente, California

ZIP CODE

Please cancel your meeting with Chung Hee Park, military-fascist-absolute dictator. Mr. Park's constitutional amendment to run for the third term has begun floor action in the National Assembly. Next week's summit talk will bring the benefit for Park only, and will result to hear the first voice of Anti-Americanism in South Korea. I hope you remember that Batista brought Castro; Chiang Kai-Shek brought Mao; and Diem brought Viet Cong.

Woo Jung Ju, Ph.D.
Professor of History

SENDER'S TEL. NO.   NAME & ADDRESS

Texas College
Tyler, Texas 75701

WU 1207 (R 5-69)

157

NO. WDS.—CL. OF SVC.	PD. OR COLL.	CASH NO.	CHARGE TO THE ACCOUNT OF	☐ OVER NIGHT TELEGRAM UNLESS BOX ABOVE IS CHECKED THIS MESSAGE WILL BE SENT AS A TELEGRAM

Send the following message, subject to the terms on back hereof, which are hereby agreed to .

APRIL 24, 1971 ___ 19

TO HON. DAE JUNG KIM

STREET & NO. NEW DEMOCRATIC PARTY'S PRESIDENTIAL CANDIDACY

CARE OF
OR APT. NO.

TELEPHONE

CITY & STATE RESIDENCE SEOUL, KOREA

ZIP CODE

YOUR VICTORY IS CERTAIN. WE HERE ADMIRE YOUR PLATFORM.

MAY GOD BLESS THE REVIVAL OF DEMOCRACY AND PEACEFUL

TRANSFER OF GOVERNMENT IN KOREA. I CONGRATULATE

YOUR CERTAIN VICTORY.

WOO JUNG JU

PROFESSOR OF HISTORY

ELIZABETH CITY STATE UNIV.

ELIZABETH CITY, N. C. 27909

SENDER'S TEL. NO.   NAME & ADDRESS

WU 1207 (R 5-69)

158

The author with Senator John W. Warner

Dr. Ju with Mrs. and Mr. Kim Dae Jung, in the backyard of Senator Edward M. Kennedy's home in McLean, VA in 1983. Kim Dae Jung was elected the President of the Republic of Korea in 1997.

160

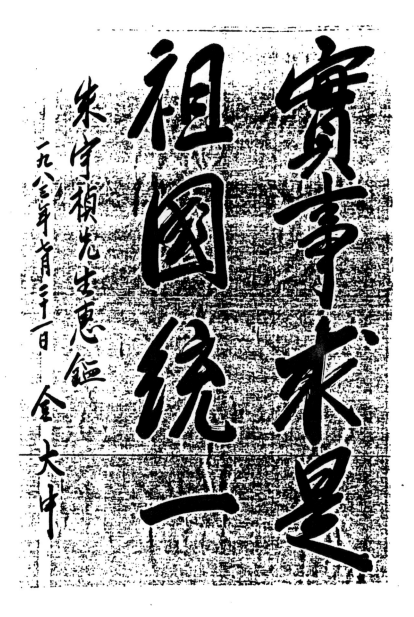

實事求是

祖國統一

朱守楨先生惠鑒

一九八三年月三十一日 金大中

한국일보 워싱톤

1999년 7월6일 (화요일)

김대중대통령 동포간담회 참석자

▲한인회 회장단:송제경 워싱톤지구 한인연합회장, 이종율 북 버지니아 한인회장, 이숙원 수도권메릴랜드 한인회장, 박평국 메릴랜드 한인회장, 장재호 리치몬드 한인회장, 김길남 미주총 연 회장, 최광수 전 미주총연 부회장.

▲동포 원로:김융순 전 가톨릭대학 경제학교수, 고흥표 전 워 싱톤한인회장.

▲사회봉사·교육분야 단체장:한광수 한글학교협의회 회장, 최경수 워싱톤한인봉사센터(KCSC) 소장, 최진희 워싱톤한인 YMCA 총무, 정인숙 가정상담소 소장.

▲주류사회진출 1.5~2세 단체:밀러김 한국계미국시민연맹 (LOKA) 회장, 마크김 한미연합회 워싱톤사무소장.

▲전문직 종사자:이덕선 Allied Technology Group 사장, 김재욱 JWK International Corp.사장, 손영환 ICT 항공·통 신산업 사장, 서홍석 전 미주의사협회장.

▲미국 공무원:정동수 상무부 수출전략실장.

▲종교계:김종철 매나사스한인침례교회 목사, 이원상 와싱톤 중앙장로교회 목사, 박문규 워싱톤무궁화교회 목사, 임승철 성 김안드레아한인천주교회 신부, 고성 한국사 스님.

▲학계·문화계:주우정 노스캐롤라이나 주립대 교수, 문범강 조지타운대학 교수(화가), 서순희 한국예술원장.

▲입양아:Jennifer Arndt 템플대 대학원생.

감사패

주식회사 박용수

귀하께서는 평소 남다른 애국애족의 정신으로 이 나라의 번영과 발전을 위하여 헌신하시는 한편 1980년 본원을 설립하시어 오늘에 이르기까지 굳건한 신념으로 온갖 정성을 다하신 그 숭고한 뜻이 길이 빛나므로 여기에 감사의 뜻을 표하나이다

1991년 4월 25일

대한노인복지 중앙회
회장 이 종 상